T0324426

HARVARD ECONOMIC STUDIES
Volume CXIV

*Awarded the David A. Wells Prize for
the year 1953–54 and published from
the income of the David A. Wells Fund.*

The studies in this series are published by the
Department of Economics of Harvard University.
The Department does not assume responsibility
for the views expressed.

Theory of MARKETS

TUN THIN

HARVARD UNIVERSITY PRESS
Cambridge, Massachusetts   1967

Second Printing

Library of Congress Catalog Card Number: 60–5398
Printed in the United States of America

Preface

This book is a revised version of a Ph.D. thesis that was submitted to Harvard University in November 1952.

In this work, a general study is made of pricing in three different markets — perfect competition, perfect monopoly, and imperfect competition. The main part of the book is, however, concerned with oligopoly. The solutions of these markets offered by Cournot, Smithies, Chamberlin, Stackelberg, Fellner, and Robinson are presented mathematically. My own version of the theory of rational pricing in oligopoly is then given. Conceptually, my solution is akin to Game Theory in that it gives a set of rules governing the behavior of the sellers for every conceivable situation.

The mathematics used in this book is elementary and involves only the elements of calculus and of matrix algebra, and the indifference curves technique, which is used for characterizing the rational behavior in the case of two sellers. Readers without training in mathematics may omit Sections 3 to 12. This study is intended for readers who have already been initiated into the theories of markets and have acquainted themselves with such basic textbooks as Chamberlin's *Theory of Monopolistic Competition* and Triffin's *Monopolistic Competition and General Equilibrium*.

I wish to express my gratitude to Professor Wassily W. Leontief for suggesting the subject matter to me and for valuable advice and suggestions, and to Dr. Carl Kaysen for reading and criticizing the manuscript. I am greatly indebted to Dr. Freddy Ba Hli, my friend and former classmate in Burma, a student at the Massachusetts Institute of Technology at the time the original thesis was written, who followed the manuscript as it evolved, chapter by chapter, and whose suggestions were many.

I am grateful to the Government of the Union of Burma for its grant of a State Scholarship which enabled me to study in the United States and to Dr. Htin Aung, the Rector, and the authorities of the University of Rangoon for their kindness in giving me a leave of absence from the University and making all other necessary facilities available.

In the revision of the original thesis, and in the preparation of the manuscript for the printers, my wife Mya Saw Shin's editorial and proofreading help has been invaluable. My thanks are also due to Mr. Martin L. Loftus, librarian of the Joint Fund-Bank Library and his assistants, Miss Narinder Kaur and Mr. James E. Jones, who very kindly and efficiently supplied me with all the materials that I requested, also to Mr. Roy E. Carlson, chief of the Graphics Section of the International Monetary Fund, and his assistants, particularly Mr. Richard D. Lawrie, for the illustrations in this book. I am also greatly indebted to my secretary, Mrs. Odette Alvord, who patiently typed and retyped the manuscript for the printers.

T.T.

International Monetary Fund
Washington, D.C.
July 1958

Contents

Theory of Markets

မွေးသမိခင်ကျေးဇူးရှင်အား

ဤစာအုပ်ဖြင့်

ကန်တော့ပန်းဆင်ပါသည်။

CHAPTER I

Introduction

1. THE PRESENT APPROACH

1.1. *The concept of "solution"*

1.1.1. In the field of economic theory, most of the solutions to problems aimed at determining certain unknown variables (such as prices and quantities) are given as point solutions each of which will give one set of values. For example, in the study of markets for commodities, labor, and money, the Theory of Demand and Supply offers the equilibrium solution which gives the prices of these commodities in perfect competition. Again, the theories of general equilibrium offer solutions deriving a set of values for the variables under consideration from some simultaneous equations. In most other cases of economic theory, such as the theory of production, the theory of welfare, the theory of imperfect competition,[1] equilibrium values of desired variables are usually obtained by the solutions of extremum (maximum or minimum) problems.

Regarding the concept of "solution," new thoughts have been raised by the Theory of Games.[2] According to this theory, a solution consists of a complete set of rules of behavior for the participants in all conceivable situations. In game theory, with each set of rules of behavior a set of imputations, that is, information as to how the total proceeds will be distributed among the participants if they behave rationally, is also given. Thus

---

[1] The theories of imperfect competition put forward by Cournot, Smithies, Chamberlin, Stackelberg, and Fellner, for example, all give single point solutions, which, in the maximizing process, introduce as constraints conjectures as to how the other sellers will behave.

[2] See J. von Neumann and O. Morgenstern, *Theory of Games and Economic Behavior* (Princeton: Princeton University Press, 1947), Section 4, pp. 31 ff.

the solution is not a single imputation but rather a system of imputations.

1.2. *The proposed oligopoly solution*

1.2.1. Although the concept of solution that is used in the oligopoly solution proposed in Chapters IV through VI is akin to game theory, the methods used in deriving the solution are different. Thus far the development in the Theory of Games has been centered in the solution of zero-sum games (where the losses of some persons in the game are equivalent to the gains of the remaining persons) and the min-max games (where with two players, though both want to maximize their gains, because it is a zero-sum game one player must have negative gains so that instead of maximizing his gains he is minimizing his losses).[3] In economics, other situations are encountered, namely, non-zero-sum and max-max games. In Sec. 13.3.5, Stackelberg's solution is expressed as a max-max game solution. A more satisfactory solution for non-zero-sum games and max-max type solutions is still needed.[4]

1.2.2. We use the indifference curves technique in the case of two sellers and the results are extended to the case of n sellers. The proofs that are given are far from rigorous but, in presenting these problems, it is hoped that the attention of mathematicians will be attracted to some of the peculiar problems of economics and that as a result new mathematical techniques will be developed to cope with the special problems.

1.2.3. In the proposed oligopoly solution, rather than giving definite sets of profits or prices for the sellers, we shall be concerned with directions only, that is, with whether the sellers will decide to increase or decrease their prices. It is to be noted here that although theories of competition or monopoly give definite points of solutions in mathematical or graphic form, in actual practice definite prices and profits cannot be determined with this procedure because demand curves, supply curves,

---

[3] See J. McKinsey, *Introduction to the Theory of Games* (New York: McGraw-Hill, 1952), pp. 358–359.

[4] See R. Dorfman, P. A. Samuelson and R. M. Solow, *Linear Programming and Economic Analysis* (New York: McGraw-Hill, 1958), pp. 444–445.

costs curves, or other data are lacking. Determination of the directions of the price movements is, therefore, the second best solution.

1.2.4. In the formulation of the oligopoly problem in this book, many explicit and implicit simplifications have been made. A few important simplifications will be mentioned in this subsection. To isolate the case of pricing from all other means of increasing the profits of a seller, it is assumed that the quality of the product and the advertising costs are kept invariant. The importance of these factors is not to be underestimated. In a country like the United States of America, the competition in products is becoming more and more pronounced. In certain industries, conjecturing what new models the other sellers will introduce is now more important than conjecturing what price the other sellers will fix. These factors are introduced, though very superficially, in Sec. 14.2.9, merely to show how the techniques given in this book can be used for other ways of increasing profits.

Nor is the problem of free exit and free entry of sellers from and into a market considered in this book. Most economists treat this problem not as the determining factor in the decision-making process of a seller but rather as affecting the end result of the solution in making average revenue equal to, or greater than, average cost. Thus this equality or inequality is not determined by a seller; rather, it is the result of the structure of the market. From the point of view of studying the behavior of the sellers, free exit and entry are unimportant. Any treatment of the exit or entry problem should involve consideration on the part of a seller (who may still be a monopolist) or of sellers in an oligopolistic market, whether their actions (changing prices or products) will induce other sellers to come into or to leave the market by increasing or decreasing its attractiveness.

The curves that are used in Chapters IV and V are oversimplified continuous curves. The analysis, however, may be adapted for discontinuous curves. In both chapters, and especially in Chapter V, the strategies that are mentioned in various situations are incomplete and more work remains to be done on the development of more strategies.

CHAPTER II

Basic Concepts

2. GENERAL DEFINITIONS

2.1. *Products and markets*

2.1. The terms that appear often in this work are defined as follows:

"Sellers" are not restricted to persons who are exclusively in the retail or distribution business. A manufacturer is also a seller when he is distributing his products. This study is concerned with the pricing of products; hence the general term "seller" is used to designate anyone who has to price his products at any level of distribution.

A "product" is a general category of goods such as coffee, automobiles, or shoes.

An "undifferentiated product" is a product, all units of which, to the buyers in the market, are identical whether they are sold by one seller or many.

A "differentiated product" is a product, all units of which, to the buyers in the market, are not identical, that is, there will be subproducts or, as we shall call them, "varieties." This differentiation between varieties may be caused by such factors as different trade-marks, different trade names, different packages or containers, or different sellers. "Differentiation" in this study will be used as Professor Chamberlin defines it:

A general class of product is differentiated if any significant basis exists for distinguishing the goods (or services) of one seller from those of another . . . Differentiation may be based upon certain characteristics of the product itself, such as exclusive patented features; trade-marks; trade names; peculiarities of the package or container, if any; or singularity in quality, design, color, or style.[1]

[1] E. H. Chamberlin, *The Theory of Monopolistic Competition*, 7th edition (Cambridge, Mass.: Harvard University Press, 1956), p. 56.

A "market" is defined to include all the sellers and buyers in a given area, selling or buying a *single product*, which may be differentiated or undifferentiated. If it is differentiated, then all its varieties and only its varieties will comprise the market. Hence there will be a market for each product.

A "general market" includes all the markets in a given area. The general theory of Walras and Pareto is a study of this general market. Mrs. Robinson's definition of industry and Professor Chamberlin's definition of a group of sellers are equivalent to our definition of market.[2]

2.2. *Perfect competition and perfect monopoly*

2.2. Historically, pricing was first studied by economists in two types of markets, "perfect competition"[3] and "perfect monopoly." In giving definitions to these two markets, economists seem to be in accord with each other on a number of points. The words "competition" and "monopoly" refer only to the number of sellers; "competition" is used to indicate the market where there is more than one seller selling a product, differentiated or undifferentiated, and "monopoly" is used to indicate the market where there is only one seller. The adjective "perfect" placed before "competition" and "monopoly"[4] indicates that the market is unalloyed in all respects. Since "Perfect monopoly" is defined as a market where there is only one seller who has complete control over the price, in "perfect competition," there must be more than one seller, and each seller must have no influence on the price.

2.3. *Imperfect competition*

2.3.1. Later, the third and the more difficult kind of market came to be studied by the economists; the cases of "imperfection"

---

[2] Both definitions are discussed in Robert Triffin, *Monopolistic Competition and General Equilibrium Theory* (Cambridge, Mass.: Harvard University Press, 1949), pp. 78–85.

[3] Since the distinction between "perfect" and "pure" competition is not relevant to our discussion, the terms are used interchangeably.

[4] Boulding uses the phrase "pure monopoly," *Economic Analysis*, Revised edition (New York: Harper, 1948), p. 523. In general, however, "monopoly," "perfect monopoly," and "pure monopoly" are used synonymously.

which we will call "imperfect competition." Here, the market is not one of "perfect monopoly," as it has more than one seller, and it is not one of "perfect competition," as the ability of an individual seller to influence or control his own price or quantity is not altogether excluded from the definition.

2.3.2. Within the general field of imperfect competition, the following three cases can be distinguished:[5] "monopolistic competition," "differentiated oligopoly," and "undifferentiated oligopoly." Professor Kenneth E. Boulding gives a concise definition of these cases, as follows:

> The four cases of competition are then defined by ringing the changes on two fundamental conditions: the homogeneity of the product and the number of firms. When many firms are producing a homogeneous product the result is perfect competition. When many firms are producing heterogeneous products, and the product of each firm is similar to but not identical with the product of other firms in the same industry, the condition is known as monopolistic competition. When a *few* firms are selling a homogeneous product there is a condition which may be called *perfect oligopoly*. When a few firms are selling heterogeneous products there is a condition which may be called *imperfect oligopoly*. Where there are only two sellers the condition is known as "duopoly." [6]

3. MONOPOLY

3.1. *Notations*

3.1. The following notations will be used in this study unless otherwise stated:

(3:A) A market is denoted by M. Should there be more than one, we write $M_1, M_2, \ldots, M_n$.

(3:B) Should there be more than one seller, sellers are numbered $1, 2, \ldots, n$.

---

[5] There are other types of classifications besides this. For example in Joel Dean's *Managerial Economics* (New York: Prentice-Hall, 1951, p. 48), Clair Wilcox gives the following classification: "There is perfect competition, pure competition, imperfect competition, monopolistic competition, non-price competition, oligopolistic competition, cutthroat or destructive competition."

[6] Boulding, pp. 569–570. Boulding's "perfect oligopoly" and "imperfect oligopoly" are equivalent to our "undifferentiated oligopoly" and "differentiated oligopoly," respectively.

(3:C) The price of a product is denoted by p. The prices charged by sellers $1, 2, \ldots, n$, are denoted by $p_1, p_2, \ldots, p_n$, respectively.

(3:D) Profits of a seller are denoted by g. The profits of sellers $1, 2, \ldots, n$, are denoted by $g_1, g_2, \ldots, g_n$, respectively.

(3:E) The costs of a seller are denoted by c, and the costs of sellers $1, 2, \ldots, n$, are denoted by $c_1, c_2, \ldots, c_n$, respectively.

(3:F) Both the function itself and the value of the function are denoted by the same symbol. For example, to represent profits as a function of price, we write $g = g(p)$, where g on the left-hand side represents the value of the function, in this case profits, and g on the right-hand side represents a functional relation. If g_1 is a function of $p_1, p_2, \ldots, p_n$, we write $g_1 = g_1(p_1, p_2, \ldots, p_n)$.

(3:G) The quantity of a product demanded in a market is denoted by x. The quantities of a product, differentiated or undifferentiated, demanded in a market from sellers $1, 2, \ldots, n$, are denoted by $x_1, x_2, \ldots, x_n$, respectively.

The demand function facing a seller i with prices as independent variables will be represented by $x_1 = x_1(p_1, p_2, \ldots, p_n)$.

The demand function facing a seller i with quantities sold by other sellers as independent variables will be represented by $p_1 = p_1(x_1, x_2, \ldots, x_n)$.

(3:H) The revenue for a seller is defined as quantity of the product sold multiplied by price and is denoted by R. Thus $R = px$. Profits equal revenue minus costs, or $g = px - c$.

3.2. *Monopoly solution as maxima of a function with one variable*

3.2.1. Given the demand and cost functions for our monopolist as $p = p(x)$ and $c = c(x)$ respectively, the profits of the monopolist can be written as

(3:I) $g = xp(x) - c(x) = \phi(x)$,
where ϕ is a function.

The problem is to find the conditions that have to be satisfied in an equilibrium position for our monopolist.[7] For such an analysis we have to make two assumptions.

---

[7] The mathematical formulation of this problem of monopoly is given in Appendix A.

(3:J) We assume that the objective of the monopolist is to maximize his profits.

(3:K) We assume also that when his profits are maximum, he is in equilibrium position.

To understand the implications of these two assumptions, let us make a graphic analysis. Let us assume that the function $g = \phi(x)$ of (3:I) takes the form shown in Fig. 1.

The assumption of (3:J) is not wholly static because it tells us that when the monopolist is in A or C, he will move toward B,

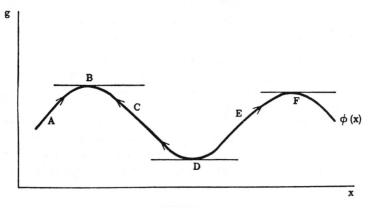

FIGURE 1

and that when he is in D, he will move toward B or F.[8] This assumption then assures us of our seller's being in equilibrium in position B or F and not in A, C, D, or E.

Of course, mathematically, the maximum points B and F are characterized by two conditions: the first, or necessary, condition is that $\partial g/\partial x = 0$; the second, or sufficient, condition is that $\partial^2 g/\partial x^2 < 0$, that is, the curve must be concave towards the horizontal axis at these points. These two conditions exclude the occurrence of the point D in equilibrium, because though point D satisfies the first condition, the second condition is not satisfied.

[8] This is demonstrated in Appendix A.

4. PERFECT COMPETITION

4.1. *General conditions for perfect competition*

4.1.1. Traditionally, perfect competition is characterized by the fact that no single seller may have power to influence the market price;[9] in order that there be perfect competition, then, a market must fulfill the following conditions:

(4:A) To the buyers, all units of the product sold by different sellers must be identical.

(4:B) There must be a large number of buyers and sellers so that the amount sold by any one seller or by several in combination is negligible.

4.1.2. Let us now study these conditions and their implications. To say that sellers are selling an identical product is to say that all units of the product and all the sellers selling this product are alike in every respect; the buyers must not prefer one unit to another because of different trade-marks, trade names, packages or containers, and so on, nor prefer one seller to another, because of personality, reputation, location, and so on. "Under such conditions it is evident that buyers and sellers will be paired in 'random' fashion in a large number of transactions. It will be entirely a matter of chance from which seller a particular buyer makes his purchase, and purchases over a period of time will be distributed among all according to the law of probability."[10]

4.1.3. Mathematically, the above definition of an "identical product" means that the following two conditions have to be satisfied.

(4:C) The total demand for the product in the market must be capable of being represented by a single demand function, such as $p = p(x)$, where p is the price and x is the total amount of the product that would be bought in the market (assuming that other factors such as prices of other products and income remain constant), and $x = x_1 + x_2 + \cdots + x_n$, where $x_1, x_2, \ldots, x_n$

---

[9] For example, Chamberlin, *Monopolistic Competition*, p. 7.
[10] Chamberlin, *Monopolistic Competition*, p. 8.

represent sales made by sellers $1, 2, \ldots, n$. We shall call this condition the necessary condition for an identical product.

(4:D) All units of the product that exist in the market in the hands of different sellers must have the same chance of being sold. For example, at a certain price p', the total amount that would be demanded is x' (given by the demand function) and if the existing amount of that product for sale in the market is S, then every unit of this amount must have the same chance x'/S of being sold to a buyer at the price p'. We shall call this the sufficient condition for an identical product.

4.1.4. To study the implications of (4:A) and (4:B), let us look at the equilibrium position of an individual seller, that is, when his profits are maximum. We will take the case of seller 1. His profits will be:

(4:1) $$g_1 = x_1 p(x) - c_1(x_1),$$

where $x = x_1 + x_2 + \cdots + x_n$.

For g_1 to be maximum, we must have:[11]

$$\frac{\partial g_1}{\partial x_i} = 0. \qquad (i = 1, 2, \ldots, n)$$

From (4:1), $\quad \dfrac{\partial g_1}{\partial x_1} = p(x) + x_1 \dfrac{\partial p}{\partial x_1} - \dfrac{\partial c_1}{\partial x_1} = 0,$

$$\frac{\partial g_1}{\partial x_2} = \qquad x_1 \frac{\partial p}{\partial x_2} \qquad = 0,$$

(4:2) $\qquad \vdots \qquad\qquad \vdots \qquad\qquad \vdots$

$$\frac{\partial g_1}{\partial x_n} = \qquad x_1 \frac{\partial p}{\partial x_n} \qquad = 0.$$

Before we study the value of the coefficient $x_1(\partial p/\partial x_i)$ with reference to condition (4:A), let us pause to look at the following mechanical analogy.

[11] See Appendix B.

4.2. *A mechanical analogy*

4.2.1. Suppose we have a coil of spring in a cylinder with a piston on top of it as shown in Fig. 2. When the piston is pressed down against the spring, the force S that is put on the spring is equal to the force of reaction x that the spring exerts on the piston. The force x of the spring depends on the height p of the coil, that is, $x = x(p)$, or in the reverse form $p = p(x)$. An elementary physical principle tells us that the more the coil is squeezed, or, in other words, the smaller the height p, the greater the force x becomes, that is, $\partial p/\partial x < 0$.

If the force S is very large, say 1000 pounds, then the question

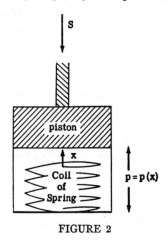

FIGURE 2

is, if a fly rests on the piston, will the piston move? Theoretically, if there is no friction between the piston and cylinder and if the function $p = p(x)$ is continuous, the piston would be displaced; but the displacement would be so small that it would require a very special measuring instrument to measure it. Let us suppose that the minimum displacement of the piston that our measuring instrument is sensitive enough to show is Δp_m, a finite quantity. Any displacement $\Delta p < \Delta p_m$ will have to be disregarded.

If p_0 and x_0 are the initial values of p and x, then, by the first approximation of Taylor's expansion,

$$p(x) = p(x_0) + (x - x_0)p'(x_0),$$

where $$p' = \frac{\partial p}{\partial x},$$

or $$p(x) - p(x_0) = \Delta x p'(x_0),$$

where $$\Delta x = x - x_0,$$

or $$p - p_0 = \Delta x p'(x_0),$$

or

(4:3) $$\Delta p = \Delta x p'(x_0),$$

where $$\Delta p = p - p_0.$$

This result will enable us to calculate Δx_m for a given Δp_m. From the initial position (p_0, x_0), if the change in the force, say Δx_α, is less than Δx_m, then Δp_α given by (4:3) is less than Δp_m, and by definition Δp_α and Δx_α may be neglected.

4.2.2. In terms of economics, we may regard x as the quantity demanded and p as the price. The function $p = p(x)$ when plotted on a graph gives a demand curve as shown in Fig. 3. Let E with coordinates (x_0, p_0) be the equilibrium point, that is, the point where the demand and supply curves intersect. Let the slope of the demand curve at E be $p'(x_0) = \tan \theta = 2 \times 10^{-6}$,

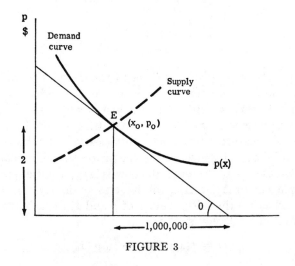

FIGURE 3

where 2 represents the price in dollars and 10^6 represents the quantity of the product.

At E, amount supplied S_0 = amount demanded x_0. The problem confronting us is to find the maximum amount Δx_m of the product that can be taken off the market without affecting the prevailing market price. We may apply the mechanical analogy and say that Δx_m would depend on the sensitivity of the market measured by Δp_m (that is, if the price change in the market is less than Δp_m, neither consumers nor sellers would consider that anything in the market had changed and would carry on as before). For this particular example, let $\Delta p_m = 1$ cent. Then we can find Δx_m for the equilibrium output x_0 as follows: For $\Delta p_m = 1/100$ dollars, we find from (4:3) that $p'(x_0)\Delta x_m = 1/100$. Substituting the value of $p'(x_0)$, as we have assumed above, $2 \times 10^{-6} \Delta x_m = 1/100$. Hence $\Delta x_m = 5000$ units of the product, that is, a change in x that is less than 5000 units would not *measurably* affect the price.

For the given sensitivity of the market Δp_m, we can thus calculate Δx_m for any point on a given demand curve. If in a market the capacity of any seller x_c (that is, the maximum quantity the seller can sell) is less than all the possible values of Δx_m, then we have the case of perfect competition, where *no single*[12] seller can affect the market price by changing his sales or by withdrawing from the market.

In the traditional theories, for the existence of perfect competition, there must be an infinite number of sellers, each of whom sells an amount which is very nearly zero — giving no minimum limit to the number of sellers and no maximum limit to the capacity of each seller. The case of perfect competition then becomes wholly imaginary, incapable of existing in the real world. We have remedied this shortcoming by defining perfect competition in terms of finite quantities.

4.3. *General equilibrium under perfect competition*

Let us assume that in the perfectly competitive market which we discussed in Secs. 4.1.3 and 4.1.4, Δp_m is given and that we

---

[12] We can substitute k sellers for one seller, in which case the capacity of each must be less than $\Delta x_m/k$.

can therefore calculate Δx_m. By the definition of perfect competition, no one seller, by varying or withdrawing his capacity output x_c, can affect the price in the market. This means that $x_c \leqq \Delta x_m$, and $x_i p'(x_0) \leqq \Delta p_m$, where $x_i \leqq x_c$. Hence $x_i p'(x_0)$ must be disregarded or dropped from consideration, that is,

$$(4:4) \qquad\qquad x_i p'(x_0) \equiv 0,$$

where $\equiv$ means "by definition is equal to."

Therefore in (4:2) all the terms involving $x_1(\partial p/\partial x_i)$ $(i = 1, 2, \ldots, n)$ disappear[13] and we are left with a single equation for seller 1, $p(x) = \partial c_1/\partial x_1$. This means that in equilibrium each seller equates his marginal cost to the market price to decide the best output. This is the condition to be fulfilled for perfect competition according to the traditional theories.

For n sellers we have n equations:

$$(4:5) \qquad\qquad p(x) = \frac{\partial c_i}{\partial x_i}. \qquad\qquad (i = 1, 2, \ldots, n)$$

These equations together with the market demand equation $p = p(x)$ can be solved for the $n + 1$ unknowns, $x_1, x_2, \ldots, x_n$, and p.

4.4. *Conjectural variation and perfect competition*

The results of (4:5) may be obtained in another way. For maximum profits of a seller, say, seller 1, we must have:

$$(4:6) \qquad\qquad \frac{\partial g_1}{\partial x_i} = 0. \qquad\qquad (i = 1, 2, \ldots, n)$$

To get the same solution as in Sec. 4.3, we will have to regard

----

[13] In (4:2), $\dfrac{\partial p}{\partial x_i} = \dfrac{\partial p}{\partial x} \cdot \dfrac{\partial x}{\partial x_i}$

$$= \frac{\partial p}{\partial x},$$

since $x = x_1 + x_2 + \cdots + x_n$.

$\partial g_1/\partial x_i$, $i \neq 1$, as being identically equal to zero.[14] The economic meaning of this is that a seller's position is not influenced by the actions of any other seller. If this condition describes our market structure, an individual seller, in trying to maximize his profits, does not concern himself with the output level of other sellers, nor does he conjecture the behavior of the other sellers. This kind of market will later be defined as having no "oligopolistic" elements.

Thus we can also say that perfect competition is present if in a market,

(i) an identical product is sold, and

(ii) there are no "oligopolistic elements" in the market.

4.5. Cournot's condition for perfect competition

4.5. Cournot[15] derives the result of (4:5) by assuming that the amount that each seller sells is negligible and can be regarded as identically equal to zero. Cournot's proof is demonstrated below.

Cournot's demand function is in the form

(4:9) $$D = F(p) \quad \text{or} \quad p = f(D),$$

where $D = D_1 + D_2 + \cdots + D_k + \cdots + D_n$, and $D_1, D_2, \ldots, D_n$ are the amounts of the commodity sold by sellers $1, 2, \ldots, n$.[16]

Each producer is subject to the cost of production expressed

---

[14] $g_1 = x_1 p(x) - c_1(x_1)$,

(4:7) $$\frac{\partial g_1}{\partial x_1} = p(x) + x_1 \cdot \frac{\partial p}{\partial x_1} - \frac{\partial c_1}{\partial x_1} = 0$$

for g_1 to be maximum.

From $$g_j = x_j p(x) - c_j(x_j), \qquad (j = 1, 2, \cdots, n)$$

(4:8) $$\frac{\partial g_j}{\partial x_1} = x_j \frac{\partial p}{\partial x_1}.$$

But $\partial g_j/\partial x_i = 0$ and, since $x_j \neq 0$, $\partial p/\partial x_1 = 0$; when we substitute in (4:7) we get $p(x) = \partial c_1/\partial x_1$.

[15] Augustin Cournot, *Researches into the Mathematical Principles of the Theory of Wealth*, 1838, translated by N. T. Bacon and Irving Fisher (New York: Macmillan, 1927).

[16] Cournot, p. 80.

by the functions[17] $\phi_1(D_1)$, $\phi_2(D_2)$, . . . $\phi_k(D_k)$, . . . $\phi_n(D_n)$; then the profit of the kth seller is

$$D_k f(D) - \phi_k(D_k),$$

and it is maximum when

$$f(D) + D_k \frac{\partial p}{\partial D} - \phi_k'(D_k) = 0,$$

where $\phi_k'(D_k) = \partial\phi_k/\partial D_k$,

or

$$p + D_k \frac{\partial p}{\partial D} - \phi_k'(D_k) = 0,$$

or

$$p \frac{\partial D}{\partial p} + D_k - \phi_k'(D_k) \frac{\partial D}{\partial p} = 0,$$

or

$$D_k + [p - \phi_k'(D_k)] \frac{\partial D}{\partial p} = 0.^{[18]}$$

Cournot then says:

The effects of competition have reached their limit, when each of the partial productions D_k is *inappreciable*, not only with reference to the total production $D = F(p)$, but also with reference to the derivative $F'(p)$, so that the partial production D_k could be subtracted from D without any appreciable variation resulting in the price of the commodity. This hypothesis is the one which is realized, in social economy, for a multitude of products, and, among them, for the most important products . . .

According to this hypothesis, in the equation

$$D_k + [p - \phi'_k(D_k)] \frac{\partial D}{\partial p} = 0,$$

the term D_k can be neglected without sensible error, which reduces the equation to

$$p - \phi_k'(D_k) = 0.^{[19]}$$

The above equation is in the same form as (4:5), and its n

[17] Cournot, p. 85.
[18] Cournot, p. 90.
[19] Cournot, p. 90.

equations together with the demand function (4:9) determine all the unknown quantities p and $D_1, D_2, \ldots, D_n$.

5. IMPERFECT COMPETITION

5.1. General concept of imperfect competition

5.1.1. In perfect competition, two conditions are always satisfied:

(5:A) An individual seller cannot influence the price of others.

(5:B) An individual seller cannot fix his own price above the market price.

In all the cases of imperfect competition defined in Sec. 2.3, we find that although one of the above conditions may be satisfied, both conditions cannot be. Section 5 is devoted to investigating when these conditions are and are not satisfied in different cases of imperfect competition.

As shown in Sec. 2.3.2, the various kinds of imperfect competition may be divided into two classes: markets where the sellers sell undifferentiated products, and those where the sellers sell differentiated products.

5.2. Imperfect competition with undifferentiated product

Obviously the first case, where sellers sell an undifferentiated product, is distinguished from perfect competition by the fact that the sellers are few. As the product is undifferentiated, (5:B) will be satisfied, because if the seller charges a price above the market price, buyers will not buy from him. Because sellers are few, (5:A) will not be present. According to the classification of Sec. 2.3.2, this case is called "undifferentiated oligopoly."

5.3. Imperfect competition with differentiated product

5.3.1. Let us now look at the market with a differentiated product. In this case, though each seller is able to set his own price independently, that is, though (5:B) is not present, "yet his market is interwoven with those of his competitors, and he is no longer to be isolated from them."[20] In other words, the amount that a seller can sell depends not only on his price but

[20] Chamberlin, *Monopolistic Competition*, p. 81.

also on the prices of other sellers. Thus for each seller, we have a demand equation expressing the sales that can be made by him as a function of the prices of all the sellers. Suppose there are n sellers in the market; the demand equations for them can be written as follows:

$$x_1 = x_1(p_1, p_2, \ldots, p_n),$$

(5:1)
$$x_i = x_i(p_1, p_2, \ldots, p_n),$$

$$x_n = x_n(p_1, p_2, \ldots, p_n).$$

Assume that these equations can also be written in the inverse form as follows:

$$p_1 = p_1(x_1, x_2, \ldots, x_n),$$

(5:2)
$$p_i = p_i(x_1, x_2, \ldots, x_n),$$

$$p_n = p_n(x_1, x_2, \ldots, x_n).$$

5.3.2. In Sec. 2.1, we defined a "differentiated product" as a product, all units of which are not identical to the buyers in the market. With this definition in mind, let us see what types of buyers will be facing each seller in the differentiated market.

Let us examine the conditions during a certain period when prices and other factors (such as the nature of advertisement and the quality of the product) do not change. In such a stationary situation in the differentiated market, we would say that every buyer is attached to his own sellers and to his own brands of products.[21] That is to say, each buyer has come to like certain brands of products or, even for the same brands, he has come to like certain sellers, and he will buy certain quantities of his brands only and from his sellers only. This situation is never found in perfect competition, where there is no such thing as attachment and it is only by chance that the buyers meet their sellers.

The question that we have to answer is, would each buyer still be attached to his own brands and sellers if other factors such as

[21] See A. J. Nichol, "The Influence of Marginal Buyers on Monopolistic Competition," *Quarterly Journal of Economics*, XLIX (1935), p. 121.

advertisement or price changed? Of course, the answer is no; otherwise we would be assuming the condition of monopoly.

Hence, in the differentiated market, the buyers do change from one brand to another, or from one seller to another, as conditions change. But the degree of attachment that the buyers have for a brand or a seller is different for different buyers.

Suppose we have n sellers $1, 2, \ldots, i, \ldots, n$. At a certain level of initial prices, say p_i^0 ($i = 1, 2, \ldots, n$), the n sellers will be selling x_i^0 amounts. Assume that other conditions remain the same. If the price of one seller, say k, rises to p_k', then some of the attached buyers will go away from k and change to other sellers or brands although there will still be some buyers left with k. As the price of k rises again, some more buyers will go away from k. At a certain high price, perhaps, there will be no buyers attached to k.

Let us now see what happens when a seller decreases his price. If p_k^0 is decreased to p_k'', then some of the attached buyers of other sellers will be detached and change to k, and the demand for k's product will be increased by a certain amount Δx_k. This would be given by the demand functions in (5:1).

The first approximation of Taylor's expansion of the system of equations (5:1) about the initial values $x_1^0, x_2^0, \ldots, x_n^0$ may be written in matrix form as follows:

$$(5:3) \quad \begin{bmatrix} \Delta x_1 \\ \cdot \\ \cdot \\ \cdot \\ \Delta x_i \\ \cdot \\ \cdot \\ \cdot \\ \Delta x_n \end{bmatrix} = \begin{bmatrix} \dfrac{\partial x_1}{\partial p_1} \cdots \dfrac{\partial x_1}{\partial p_i} \cdots \dfrac{\partial x_1}{\partial p_n} \\ \cdot \quad \cdot \quad \cdot \\ \cdot \quad \cdot \quad \cdot \\ \cdot \quad \cdot \quad \cdot \\ \dfrac{\partial x_i}{\partial p_1} \cdots \dfrac{\partial x_i}{\partial p_i} \cdots \dfrac{\partial x_i}{\partial p_n} \\ \cdot \quad \cdot \quad \cdot \\ \cdot \quad \cdot \quad \cdot \\ \cdot \quad \cdot \quad \cdot \\ \dfrac{\partial x_n}{\partial p_1} \cdots \dfrac{\partial x_n}{\partial p_i} \cdots \dfrac{\partial x_n}{\partial p_n} \end{bmatrix} \begin{bmatrix} \Delta p_1 \\ \cdot \\ \cdot \\ \cdot \\ \Delta p_i \\ \cdot \\ \cdot \\ \cdot \\ \Delta p_n \end{bmatrix},$$

where $\Delta x_i = (x_i - x_i^0)$, and $\Delta p_i = (p_i - p_i^0)$.

From (5:3) we know that the changes in the demand for seller i caused by change in price p_k by Δp_k is given by

$$(5:4) \qquad \Delta x_i = \frac{\partial x_i}{\partial p_k} \Delta p_k \qquad (i = 1, 2, \ldots, n)$$

5.3.3. To find out whether (5:A) is satisfied or not in the case of imperfect competition with differentiated products, let us divide the case into two subclasses, as Chamberlin does, namely, one with few sellers and the other with a very large number of sellers. According to our terminology (Sec. 2.3.2), the case with few sellers is called differentiated oligopoly and the case with a large number of sellers is called monopolistic competition.

5.3.4. In the case of a large number of sellers, Chamberlin assumes that

any adjustment of price . . . by a single producer spreads its influence over so many of his competitors that the impact felt by any one is negligible and does not lead him to any readjustment of his own situation. A price cut, for instance, which increases the sales of him who made it, draws inappreciable amounts from the markets of each of his many competitors, achieving a considerable result for the one who cut, but without making incursions upon the market of any single competitor sufficient to cause him to do anything he would not have done anyway.[22]

This is to be interpreted to mean that in monopolistic competition (5:A) is present. Professor Triffin interprets[23] this statement as meaning that $\partial R_i/\partial p_j$ (where R denotes revenue) or $\partial x_i/\partial p_j$ "is of insignificant size, with respect to the other elements of the profit maximization calculations of the seller."

By analogy with the treatment of perfect competition given in 4.2., the case of monopolistic competition may be treated as follows:

Let us first consider the effects on seller i, when the price of a seller varies. The impact on the sales of i is given by

$$(5:4) \qquad \Delta x_i = \frac{\partial x_i}{\partial p_k} \Delta p_k.$$

---

[22] Chamberlin, *Monopolistic Competition*, p. 83.

[23] Triffin, pp. 100–102. Triffin uses q to denote quantities and he defines q as "quantities of sales."

If $\partial x_i/\partial p_k$ is not equal to zero, Δx_i must be some finite quantity. The question now is, when can Δx_i be regarded as insignificant?

Obviously, it is up to the seller i to decide whether Δx_i is significant or not. We will not be far wrong if we assume that our seller would regard the change in his sales Δx_i significant or not only as it affects his profits. Suppose the seller regards a change in his profits of less than $\Delta g_{i,m}$ as negligible. Then any change in his sales that would affect his profits by less than the amount $\Delta g_{i,m}$ can be regarded as negligible. We can represent this situation mathematically if we let the profits of seller i be given by

$$g_i = p_i x_i - c_i(x_i) = \theta(x_i),$$

where θ is a function. The first approximation of Taylor's expansion of this function about the initial output $x_i{}^0$ gives us

(5:5) $$\Delta g_i = \Delta x_i \theta'(x_i{}^0),$$

where $\Delta g_i = g_i - g_i{}^0$, $\theta' = \partial\theta/\partial x_i$, and $\Delta x_i = x_i - x_i{}^0$.

This relation enables us to calculate $\Delta x_{i,m}$ corresponding to the given $\Delta g_{i,m}$. According to the assumption above, any change in i's sales that is less than $\Delta x_{i,m}$ may be regarded as negligible.

Suppose in (5:4), the value of $\partial x_i/\partial p_k$ is such that for any change in Δp_k, however large it may be (that is, even if we write p_k for Δp_k), $\Delta x_i \leqq \Delta x_{i,m}$, then we may write

(5:6) $$\frac{\partial x_i}{\partial p_k} p_k \equiv 0.$$

As p_k is a finite quantity, we may also say, as Professor Triffin does, that sellers regard $\partial x_i/\partial p_k$ as identically equal to zero.

5.3.5. It is shown below that condition (5:A) or (5:6), which is the same thing, does not hold true for all markets with a large number of sellers in imperfect competition. As mentioned in Sec. 5.3.2, when the price of a seller increases, some of his buyers will become detached and be distributed among other sellers. Let us now take, for demonstration, an example where a significant percentage of sales, say 50 percent, will become detached from a seller. If there are many sellers, say 1000, in the market, the increase in the sales of the remaining sellers would be very small and may be regarded as insignificant, assuming

(5:7:a) that initial sales are about evenly distributed among the sellers, and

(5:7:b) that the sales that are detached, in this case 50 percent of the sales of the seller who increases his price, are also evenly distributed among the remaining sellers.

Thus when the price is increased and there is a large number of sellers, (5:A) or its equivalent (5:6) is valid.

Let us now see what happens when the seller decreases his price. Because of the decrease, sales of other sellers are detached. If we assume, as above, that 50 percent of the sales of each seller would be detached and if we assume also that the seller who cuts his price has the capacity to fulfill all the detached sales of the remaining sellers, we would conclude that the cut in price made by one seller has significant effects on the remaining sellers even if the number of sellers is large. Hence in this case, for (5:A) or (5:6) to be true, we must either

(5:8:a) restrict the capacity of the sellers, or

(5:8:b) assume that an insignificant percentage of sales becomes detached from each remaining seller when any single seller decreases his price.

5.3.6. Under the conditions given in Sec. 5.3.5, depending on whether $\partial x_i/\partial p_k$ is being regarded by seller i as negligible or not in consequence of a change in the price of k, we can distinguish between the cases of many sellers and few sellers. A similar observation can be made of perfect competition. There every seller of a product sells very small quantities and his limited capacity prevents him from absorbing significant quantities from other sellers even if he lowers his price significantly. In this case also, we have $\partial x_i/\partial p_k \equiv 0$. It is to be noted that

(5:9:a) the result is not derived directly from the demand function but from the assumption that the capacity of each seller is very, very small, and

(5:9:b) x_i does not signify the change in demand for seller i, but rather it signifies the change in the sales of seller i. To make this distinction let us use s_i rather than x_i[24] for such cases and say that

(5:10) $$\partial s_i / \partial p_k \equiv 0.$$

5.4. *Structural dependence as a subsidiary condition*

5.4.1. To study the interdependence among the sellers in imperfect competition, let us take the case of two sellers selling an identical product in the market. The profits of the sellers may be written as follows:

(5:11) $$g_1 = x_1 p(x_1 + x_2) - c_1(x_1),$$
$$g_2 = x_2 p(x_1 + x_2) - c_2(x_2).$$

Because of the nature of the demand function, both g_1 and g_2 are dependent on x_1 and x_2. From Sec. 4.4, we find that there is a solution if $\partial g_1 / \partial x_2$ and $\partial g_2 / \partial x_1$ are each identically equal to zero, that is, if there is no relation between x_1 and x_2. In this section we assume that the two are interdependent. The first seller has the power to vary only x_1, and the second seller has the power to vary only x_2; hence for seller 1 to determine his output, he must be given x_2 by the structure of the market itself or he has to conjecture it. If x_2 is known by either means, g_1 becomes a function of x_1 alone and equating $\partial g_1 / \partial x_1$ to 0 would give our seller maximum profits. The same holds true for seller 2.

5.4.2. If the sales and profits of the two sellers are dependent on one another because of the structure of the market itself, we shall call such dependence "structural." As an example of structural dependence, let us suppose that the two sellers always have the same chance of selling the product in the market, i.e., at a given price level, seller 1 can sell $\frac{1}{2}$ of the market demand and so can seller 2. Under such a condition, (5:11) becomes

(5:12:a) $$g_1 = \tfrac{1}{2} x p(x) - c_1(x_1),$$

[24] Triffin defines his quantities as "quantities of sales" and, as he does not specifically relate them to a demand function, it may be assumed that his q and our s are identical. In cases where a seller has the capacity to sell the amount that is demanded, it is immaterial whether x (derived from the demand function) or s (actual sales) is used.

(5:12:b) $$g_2 = \tfrac{1}{2}xp(x) - c_2(x_2).$$

For maximum profits,

(5:13:a) $$\frac{\partial g_1}{\partial x_1} = \tfrac{1}{2}p(x) + \tfrac{1}{2}xp'(x) - c_1'(x_1) = 0,$$

(5:13:b) $$\frac{\partial g_2}{\partial x_2} = \tfrac{1}{2}p(x) + \tfrac{1}{2}xp'(x) - c_2'(x_2) = 0.$$

If the cost functions are identical, the equations in (5:13) together with the demand equation $p = p(x_1 + x_2)$ can be solved for x_1, x_2 and p, and in equilibrium $x_1 = x_2$. In such a case, where the structural dependence between the sellers in a market is given, it is not necessary for sellers to make conjectures. The conditions that are assumed to exist in the case of perfect competition may be regarded as one example of structural dependence.

5.4.3. If the two cost functions are not identical,[25] the equations in (5:13) would give different equilibrium prices for the two sellers; the one with lower costs, say seller 1, would be able to sell at a lower price. Then the seller with the lower costs would set the price and the seller with the higher costs would be forced to charge the same price, as otherwise, buyers would leave him and buy from a lower-price firm.

5.5. Conjectural dependence[26]

5.5.1. When a seller conjectures what other sellers would do, his conjecture is based on some data. We will consider only a few of the many forms that the data can take.[27]

Let $\bar{x}_2$ represent the quantity that seller 1 thinks 2 would sell; $\bar{x}_1$ the quantity that seller 2 thinks 1 would sell; x_1^0 and x_2^0 the quantities sold by 1 and 2 in the present period; and x_1 and x_2 the quantities that 1 and 2 would sell in the next period.

Then $\bar{x}_2$ may be assumed to depend on any or all of the following: x_1, x_1^0, x_2^0, and $\bar{x}_1$ may be assumed to depend on x_2, x_1^0, x_2^0.

[25] See Boulding, p. 583, for a graphic analysis of this case.
[26] See Chapter VI below for criticisms of this kind of conjecture.
[27] See Section 8 below.

These functions expressing conjectural dependence give the subsidiary relation needed to solve the problem of maximization of profits in imperfect competition.

5.5.2. If prices instead of quantities are the independent variables, then conjectural dependence would be expressed by letting $\bar{p}_2$ represent the price that seller 1 thinks 2 would charge, $\bar{p}_1$ the price that seller 2 thinks 1 would charge, p_1^0 and p_2^0 the present prices charged by 1 and 2, and p_1 and p_2 the prices that would be charged by 1 and 2 in the next period.

Then $\bar{p}_2$ may be assumed to depend on any or all of the following: p_1, p_1^0, p_2^0, and $\bar{p}_1$ may be assumed to depend on p_2, p_1^0, p_2^0.

5.5.3. Let us now study the implications of these various forms of conjecture. First we will take the case in which prices are the independent variables. Profits are then functions of prices, as follows:

(5:14:a) $$g_1 = g_1(p_1, p_2),$$

(5:14:b) $$g_2 = g_2(p_1, p_2).$$

Let the conjectures of sellers 1 and 2 take the following form:

(5:15:a) $$\bar{p}_2 = f_1(p_1),$$

(5:15:b) $$\bar{p}_1 = f_2(p_2).$$

If we substitute $\bar{p}_2$ of (5:15:a) for p_2 of (5:14:a), g_1 becomes a function of p_1 alone, and seller 1 needs to set $\partial g_1/\partial p_1$ equal to 0 to obtain maximum profits. By using (5:14:b) and (5:15:b), we can solve for $\bar{p}_1$ and p_2. Four equations thus give us four unknowns. If p_1 is not equal to $\bar{p}_1$, and p_2 not equal $\bar{p}_2$, the market is not in equilibrium. The sellers will have to change their conjectures, that is, *new* values will have to be obtained in (5:15:a and b). After a number of approximations, the required equilibrium is sometimes, though not inevitably, reached.

5.5.4. Another form of conjecture is possible:

(5:16:a) $$\bar{p}_2 = f_1(p_1, p_2^0),$$

(5:16:b) $$\bar{p}_1 = f_2(p_1^0, p_2).$$

Substituting $\bar{p}_2$ of (5:16:a) for p_2 in (5:14:a), we obtain g_1 as a function of p_1 and $p_2{}^0$. If we set $\partial g_1/\partial p_1$ equal to 0, one variable is solved as a function of another variable, that is,

$$(5:17:a) \qquad\qquad p_1 = R_1(p_2{}^0).$$

Similarly from (5:16:b) and (5:14:b), we obtain another function,

$$(5:17:b) \qquad\qquad p_2 = R_2(p_1{}^0).$$

Each of these functions gives the price at which one seller will sell when the other seller's present price is given. These functions are called "reaction functions" and can be solved for equilibrium prices p_1 and p_2.

5.5.5. If we have more than two sellers, we use the same method to arrive at the solutions. The following formulations are based on four sellers:

$$(5:18) \qquad \begin{aligned} g_1 &= g_1(p_1, p_2, p_3, p_4), \\ g_2 &= g_2(p_1, p_2, p_3, p_4), \\ g_3 &= g_3(p_1, p_2, p_3, p_4), \\ g_4 &= g_4(p_1, p_2, p_3, p_4). \end{aligned}$$

Since seller can vary only his price, he needs three subsidiary conditions. For example, seller 1 needs conditions such that

$$\begin{aligned} {}_1\bar{p}_2 &= f_1(p_1, p_2{}^0, p_3{}^0, p_4{}^0), \\ {}_1\bar{p}_3 &= f_2(p_1, p_2{}^0, p_3{}^0, p_4{}^0), \\ {}_1\bar{p}_4 &= f_3(p_1, p_2{}^0, p_3{}^0, p_4{}^0), \end{aligned}$$

where $p_2{}^0$, $p_3{}^0$, and $p_4{}^0$ are the present prices of sellers 2, 3, and 4 and ${}_i\bar{p}_j$ is the price that i expects j to fix.

Substituting ${}_1\bar{p}_2$ for p_2, ${}_1\bar{p}_3$ for p_3, and ${}_1\bar{p}_4$ for p_4 in the first equation of (5:18), we have g_1 as a function of p_1, $p_2{}^0$, $p_3{}^0$, and $p_4{}^0$; equating $\partial g_1/\partial p_1$ to zero, we can solve p as a function of other variables, that is,

$$p_1 = R_1(p_2{}^0, p_3{}^0, p_4{}^0).$$

This is the reaction function of seller 1. Given the subsidiary equations for other sellers, we can derive three other reaction functions for sellers 2, 3, and 4, and these four reaction functions can be solved for the four unknowns p_1, p_2, p_3, p_4. In equilibrium $p_j = {}_i\bar{p}_j$.

6. ELASTICITY CLASSIFICATION OF PERFECT COMPETITION, IMPERFECT COMPETITION, AND PERFECT MONOPOLY

6.1. *General remarks*

6.1.1. Given a functional relationship $x_i = x_i(p_i)$, expressing the quantity demanded of seller i as a function of his price, we can write coefficient of elasticity of demand either as

$$(6\text{:}1) \qquad \frac{\Delta x_i}{\Delta p_i} \cdot \frac{p_i}{x_i},$$

where Δx_i and Δp_i are very small but finite quantities, or

$$(6\text{:}2) \qquad \frac{\partial x_i}{\partial p_i} \cdot \frac{p_i}{x_i},$$

where $\partial x_i / \partial p_i$ represents a derivative.

6.1.2. If in an imperfectly competitive market we have n sellers selling a differentiated product and the demand function for seller i is given by $x_i = x_i(p_1, p_2, \ldots, p_i, p_j \ldots, p_n)$, our elasticity coefficients are written as follows:

$$(6\text{:}3) \qquad \frac{\Delta x_i}{\Delta p_j} \cdot \frac{p_j}{x_i},$$

for $i = j$ and $i \neq j$, or

$$(6\text{:}4) \qquad \frac{\partial x_i}{\partial p_j} \cdot \frac{p_j}{x_i},$$

for $i = j$ and $i \neq j$.

The cross-elasticity coefficients[28] were first used by Professor Triffin, to give "a clear-cut classification of the various types of competition between sellers."[29]

[28] Coefficients in (6:3) and (6:4) are called cross-elasticity coefficients, when $i \neq j$.
[29] Triffin, p. 102.

Following Professor Triffin, there have been many articles on this subject but we will consider only those of Triffin and Fellner.

6.2. *Professor Triffin's classification*[30]

6.2.1. The first case that Professor Triffin considers is "homogeneous competition," where the firms are selling the "same" commodity. For sellers to be selling the *same* commodity, according to him, the following conditions must be fulfilled:

(6:A) "The slightest cut in p_j, p_i remaining unchanged, or

(6:B) the slightest rise in p_i, p_j remaining unchanged, reduces to zero the sales (and revenue) of i, driving all its customers toward firm j."[31]

Then the elasticity coefficient $(\Delta x_i/\Delta p_j)(p_j/x_i)$ equals infinity[32] and "depending on the number of firms between which such a relation exists, the case would be classified as duopoly, oligopoly, [or] pure competition."[33]

6.2.2. Conditions (6:A) and (6:B) will not assure that sales of i will be reduced to zero unless the two conditions are accompanied by a third one expressing the initial condition, namely,

(6:C) that the initial prices p_i^0 be equal to p_j^0. If there are more than two sellers, their prices must all be equal to the market price p^0. Then conditions (6:A) and (6:B) would read: x_i will be zero if (6:A) new price $p_j' < p_j^0$ and p_i^0 remains unchanged, that is, $\Delta p_j < 0$ and $\Delta p_i = 0$, or (6:B) new price $p_i' > p_i^0$ and p_j^0 remains unchanged, that is, $\Delta p_i > 0$ and $\Delta p_j = 0$.

6.2.3. According to (6:A) and (6:B), when p_i or p_j changes, sales of i, that is, the new sales at new prices, are reduced to zero. In the coefficient (6:3), x_i must therefore be written as x_i' to denote that it signifies the new level. It would then read

[30] Triffin, pp. 99–107.
[31] Triffin, p. 103.
[32] In his original coefficient $(\partial q_i/\partial p_i)(p_i/q_i)$, we substitute x for q and as small changes are considered we substitute Δx_i and Δp_j for ∂x_i and ∂p_j.
[33] Triffin, p. 103.

(6:3:a)
$$\frac{\Delta x_i}{\Delta p_j} \cdot \frac{p_j}{x_i + \Delta x_i}$$

or

(6:3:b)
$$\frac{\Delta x_i}{\Delta p_j} \cdot \frac{p_j}{x_i'},$$

when $x_i' = x_i + \Delta x_i$. This is an arc elasticity coefficient.[34]

6.2.4. Let us assume for the time being that (6:C) is satisfied; the conditions (6:A) and (6:B) may represent different markets. Condition (6:A) states that a price cut by j would turn the customers of i towards j and thus implicitly assumes that j's capacity can be expanded. This type of market precludes the conventional type of perfect competition, which assumes that a seller's capacity output is so insignificant that even if he cuts his price below the market price, he will not be able to absorb the sales of other sellers and thus other sellers would be left unaffected. Symbolically, it means (6:5) that in perfect competition if $\Delta p_j < 0$ and $\Delta x_i = 0$, then $(\Delta x_i/\Delta p_j)(p_j/x_i) = 0$.[35] On the other hand (6:B) can admit the assumption of this perfect competition type.

6.2.5. It is also to be noted that if we apply (6:A), $(\Delta x_i/\Delta p_j)$ $(p_j/x_i) = \infty$ is true only for $\Delta p_j < 0$ and not true for $\Delta p_j > 0$, because if we have $\Delta p_j > 0$, $x_i' \neq 0$, and the coefficient is not equal to ∞.

6.2.6. Condition (6:B) cannot be expressed by the coefficient $(\Delta x_i/\Delta p_j)(p_j/x_i)$ because the condition relates sales and change in price of the same seller. If this condition is to be used, we can use the coefficient $(\Delta x_i/\Delta p_i)(p_i/x_i)$, and for "homogeneous competition," this coefficient would be equal to infinity.

6.2.7. Triffin's second case is that of perfect monopoly, where the "sales of i would be entirely unaffected by any change in the price charged by firm j. The value of the coefficient $(\Delta x_i/\Delta p_j)(p_j/x_i)$ would be 0, and no competition at all would be present between i and j."[36] But in Sec. 6.2.4, it is shown that

[34] See Boulding, p. 141; (6:3:a) is equivalent to Boulding's type (iii).
[35] According to the notation suggested in 5.3.6, Δx_i and x_i should be written Δs_i and s_i, respectively.
[36] Triffin, p. 103.

this relation implies a conventional, perfectly competitive market. Hence the criterion does not give a clear-cut distinction between different markets.

6.2.8. The third case is that of "heterogeneous competition," where the coefficient takes a finite value. In this case "a cut in p_j, p_i remaining unchanged, or a raise in p_i, p_j remaining unchanged, affects the volume of i's sales without reducing it to zero."[37] Though only a cut in p_j is mentioned, a raise in p_j would give the same result, that is, the coefficient is valid for $\Delta p_j \gtrless 0$.

6.2.9. Thus in perfect monopoly and in imperfect competition, the coefficient is valid for $\Delta p_j \gtrless 0$, whereas in perfect competition it is valid only for $\Delta p_j < 0$. Moreover, though condition (6:C) must be satisfied for perfect competition, it need not be satisfied in the other two cases. Hence, because of different subsidiary conditions that are attached to this coefficient for different market types, comparison of the values of the coefficients of different cases would not be valid, for such a procedure would be like comparing a country's national income for different years computed at different price levels.

6.2.10. Professor Triffin introduces a subclassification in his cases of "homogeneous competition" and "heterogeneous competition." "Where the firms are in competition (as against the case of isolated selling) their interrelationship may, or may not, involve oligopolistic elements of indeterminacy . . . Oligopolistic difficulties will arise if both of the following conditions are realized:

"(1) the firm i is submitted to the competition of other firms j,"[38] that is, (6:3) is significantly different from zero,

"(2) some of these firms j that influence i are themselves affected by the changes in the price-output policy of firm i,"[39] that is, $(\Delta p_j/\Delta x_i)(x_i/p_j)$ is also significantly different from zero.

From this stipulation we infer that if the coefficients (6:3) and $(\Delta p_j/\Delta x_i)(x_i/p_j)$ are insignificantly different from zero or if they are, let us say, nearly zero, there would be no oligopolistic diffi-

---

[37] Triffin, p. 103. $(\Delta p_j/\Delta x_1)(x_i/p_j)$ is also significantly different from zero.
[38] Triffin, p. 104.
[39] Triffin, p. 104.

culties. Let us take the cases of "non-oligopolistic heterogeneous competition," and "non-oligopolistic homogeneous competition." For the first case, as it is non-oligopolistic, $(6:3) = 0$, and as it is heterogeneous competition, $(6:3) \neq 0$.[40] For the second case, condition $(6:3) = 0$ because the market is non-oligopolistic and[41] $(6:3) = \infty$ because the competition is homogeneous. Neither pair of conditions can be satisfied, for they are obviously contradictory.

6.3. *Professor Fellner's classification*[42]

6.3.1. Professor Fellner also uses cross-elasticities to classify different markets, and his classification is a modification of Professor Triffin's. Professor Fellner distinguishes between the effect on a particular firm of price changes made by a single firm and those made by a group of firms. Thus we have two types of coefficients of elasticity:

$$(6:6) \qquad \frac{\Delta x_i}{\Delta p_g} \cdot \frac{p_g}{x_i},$$

$$(6:7) \qquad \frac{\Delta x_i}{\Delta p_j} \cdot \frac{p_j}{x_i},$$

where p_g represents the price charged by "some definable group of firms" other than firm i. It is to be noted that the "quantity" as defined by Fellner means the quantity demanded, and hence it is to be inferred that it is derived from a demand function.

We shall regard p_g and Δp_g merely as shorthand notations for the phrases "price charged by a group of firms," and "change in the price charged by a group of firms," respectively.[43]

6.3.2. If the conditions

[40] See Sec. 6.2.8.

[41] See Sec. 6.2.1.

[42] William Fellner, *Competition among the Few* (New York; Knopf, 1949), pp. 50–54.

[43] In perfect competition, as only one price can prevail, p_g may be regarded as the market price. Hence the coefficient $(\Delta x_i/\Delta p_g)(p_g/x_i)$ can also be expressed in a derivative form as $(\partial x_i/\partial p_g)(p_g/x_i)$. But in imperfect competition there may be various prices in the market and as $x_i = x_i(p_1, p_2, \ldots, p_n)$, the coefficient in derivative form has no meaning.

(6:8)
$$\frac{\Delta x_i}{\Delta p_g} \cdot \frac{p_g}{x_i} = \infty,$$

(6:9)
$$\frac{\Delta x_i}{\Delta p_j} \cdot \frac{p_j}{x_i} = 0^{44}$$

are fulfilled, Professor Fellner defines the market to be perfectly competitive.

The observations made in Sec. 6.2.2 are valid in this case too; those in Sec. 6.2.4, however, do not apply. The assumption of the conventional, perfectly competitive market that each seller sells an insignificant amount can be admitted into the present definition, for in this case $x_i = 0$ because p_g (the market price) has decreased. It is to be noted that (6:8) is valid only when $\Delta p_g < 0$ and (6:9) is valid only if Δx_i and x_i refer to quantities sold and not quantities demanded.[45]

6.3.3. According to Professor Fellner, perfect monopoly exists if the following two conditions are satisfied:

(6:10)
$$\frac{\Delta x_i}{\Delta p_g} \cdot \frac{p_g}{x_i} = 0,$$

(6:11)
$$\frac{\Delta x_i}{\Delta p_j} \cdot \frac{p_j}{x_i} = 0.$$

The addition of condition (6:10) makes a clear-cut distinction between perfect competition and perfect monopoly, and eliminates the criticism made in 6.2.7.

6.3.4. Professor Fellner states that imperfect competition with a large number of sellers, that is, monopolistic competition, exists if two conditions are satisfied, namely, if

(6:12)
$$\frac{\Delta x_i}{\Delta p_g} \cdot \frac{p_g}{x_i} \text{ is finite}$$

and

(6:13)
$$\frac{\Delta x_i}{\Delta p_j} \cdot \frac{p_j}{x_i} = 0.^{[46]}$$

[44] What Fellner said was that (6:9) is neither finite nor infinite and hence we inferred that (6:9) is zero.

[45] See Sec. 6.2.4.

[46] As in (6:9), the coefficient is defined by Fellner as neither finite nor infinite.

6.3.5. He further states that for imperfect competition with a small number of sellers,

(6:14) when there is no product differentiation, the coefficient (6:7) $= \infty$,[47] and

(6:15) when there is product differentiation, the coefficient (6:7) should be finite.

6.4. *Concluding remarks*

6.4.1. The use of elasticity coefficients for the classification of different markets is not satisfactory because different qualifications have to be made to make them applicable to different markets. If we want to make use of them at all, however, the following conditions can be used to define different types of markets.

For perfect competition,

$$\frac{\Delta x_i}{\Delta p_g} \cdot \frac{p_g}{x_i + \Delta x_i} = \infty,$$

and

$$\frac{\Delta s_i}{\Delta p_j} \cdot \frac{p_j}{s_i} = 0,$$

where p_g represents market price, $\Delta p_g < 0$, $p_i^0 = p_g^0 = p_j^0 =$ initial prices, and $\Delta p_i = 0$, $\Delta p_j \gtrless 0$.

For perfect monopoly,

$$(6:6) = 0,$$
$$(6:7) = 0,$$

where $\Delta p_g \gtrless 0$, $\Delta p_j \gtrless 0$, and there is no limitation on initial conditions.

For imperfect competition with product differentiation and a large number of sellers, namely, monopolistic competition,

$$(6:6) \text{ is finite,}$$
$$(6:7) = 0,$$

[47] As i and j are defined as any two sellers in the market, we need not give the statement as Fellner does, that $(\Delta x_i/\Delta p_j)(p_j/x_i) = (\Delta x_j/\Delta p_i)(p_i/x_j) = \infty$.

and the subsidiary conditions are the same as in perfect monopoly.

For imperfect competition without product differentiation and with a small number of sellers,

$$\frac{\Delta x_i}{\Delta p_j} \cdot \frac{p_j}{x_i + \Delta x_i} = \infty,^{48}$$

where the initial prices $p_i^0 = p_o^0 = p_j^0$, $\Delta p_j < 0$, and $\Delta p_i = 0$.

For imperfect competition with product differentiation and a small number of sellers,

$$(6:7) \text{ is finite,}$$

and the subsidiary conditions are the same as in perfect monopoly.

6.4.2. We have classified the different markets in Secs. 4 and 5 by using partial derivatives; from (4:4) we find that for perfect competition,

$$x_i \frac{\partial p}{\partial x_i} \equiv 0$$

and from (5:6) we find that for monopolistic competition,

$$\frac{\partial x_i}{\partial p_k} p_k \equiv 0.$$

For the case of perfect competition, rewriting the coefficient (6:4) to read $(\partial x_i/\partial p)(p/x_i)$, where p is the market price,

$$(\partial x_i/\partial p)(p/x_i) = \frac{p}{x_i(\partial p/\partial x_i)}$$

$$= \frac{p}{0} \text{ from } (4:4)$$

$$= \infty$$

This result is the same as the first condition in Sec. 6.4.1. For the case of monopolistic competition,

[48] For uniformity, we can use the arc cross-elasticity for every case. Here, however, it is used only for those cases in which no other form is applicable.

$$\frac{\partial x_i}{\partial p_j} \cdot \frac{p_j}{x_i} = \frac{(\partial x_i/\partial p_j)p_j}{x_i}$$

$$= \frac{0}{x_i}$$

$$= 0.$$

This result is the same as the second condition for monopolistic competition in Sec. 6.4.1.

CHAPTER III

Various Solutions for the Market with Imperfect Competition

7. NATURE OF THE TREATMENT GIVEN TO THE VARIOUS SOLUTIONS IN THIS CHAPTER, AND THE CASE OF COURNOT

7.1. *Discussion of the treatment of the various solutions*

7.1. Although Professors Chamberlin and Fellner have treated extensively almost all the cases that are discussed in this chapter, there are a number of reasons for their appearance here also. First, the theories are presented in mathematical form. Second, because it was contended in Secs. 5.4 and 5.5 that the conjectural variations of the sellers in imperfect competition supply the necessary subsidiary conditions for the solution of the problem of maximization, this chapter will indicate the subsidiary conditions of various authors and show how they may be applied to arrive at solutions mathematically. My criticisms of these theories are reserved for Chapter VI.

7.2. *The case of Cournot*[1]

7.2. Cournot assumes that there are two sellers in a market selling an undifferentiated product and that the total market demand for the product may therefore be represented by a single demand function, say $p = p(x_1 + x_2)$, where p denotes the market price and x_1 and x_2 denote the sales of sellers 1 and 2,

---

[1] Augustin Cournot, *Researches into the Mathematical Principles of the Theory of Wealth*, 1838, translated by N. T. Bacon and Irving Fisher (New York: Macmillan, 1927), Chapter VII.

respectively. It is also assumed that there is no cost of production. Profits of sellers 1 and 2 are given by the following equations:

(7:1:a) $$g_1 = x_1 p(x_1 + x_2),$$

(7:1:b) $$g_2 = x_2 p(x_1 + x_2).$$

The problem is to maximize g_1 and g_2, which are functions of both x_1 and x_2. Cournot assumes that each seller conjectures that the other seller will sell in the next period the same quantity that he sells at present. This conjectural variation gives us the necessary subsidiary condition.

Let $\bar{x}_1$ represent the quantity that seller 2 thinks 1 will sell in the next period and similarly let $\bar{x}_2$ represent the quantity that seller 1 thinks 2 will sell in the next period. (7:1:a and b) may then be rewritten in the following way:

(7:2:a) $$g_1 = x_1 p(x_1 + \bar{x}_2),$$

(7:2:b) $$g_2 = x_2 p(\bar{x}_1 + x_2).$$

The problem now is to maximize g_1 and g_2, with the following subsidiary conditions,

(7:3:a) $$\bar{x}_2 = x_2{}^0,$$

(7:3:b) $$\bar{x}_1 = x_1{}^0,$$

where $x_1{}^0$ and $x_2{}^0$ represent the present quantities sold by 1 and 2. To solve the problem, we substitute $\bar{x}_2$ of (7:3:a) in (7:2:a) and derive g_1 as a function of x_1 and a parameter $x_2{}^0$. Equating $\partial g_1 / \partial x_1$ to zero, we have a function $x_1 = R_1(x_2{}^0)$, which is called the reaction function of 1. The values of x_1 given by this reaction function, corresponding to the given values of $x_2{}^0$, would give seller 1 maximum profits for the given sales of seller 2. Similarly we derive a reaction function for 2 from equations (7:3:b) and (7:2:b) and by equating $\partial g_2 / \partial x_2$ to zero. This reaction function will be in the form $x_2 = R_2(x_1{}^0)$. These two reaction functions can then be solved for x_1 and x_2, and in equilibrium $x_1 = x_1{}^0 = \bar{x}_1$ and $x_2 = x_2{}^0 = \bar{x}_2$.

This solution is the same type as that of Sec. 5.5.3, but here we substitute quantities for prices.

8. PROFESSOR SMITHIES' CASE

Professor Smithies in his two articles on imperfect competition studies a market with two sellers[2] and a market with more than two sellers,[3] the products of the sellers being differentiated in both cases.

These two cases fit perfectly our general types of conjectural dependence described in Secs. 5.5.4 and 5.5.5, respectively. The functions used in these articles are of the same type as those in the above-mentioned sections of this work, except that they take a specific form and all are linear except the cost function. We will take the case with two sellers. The demand functions are:

$$(8:1:a) \qquad x_1 = a_1 p_1 + b_1 p_2 + c_1,$$

$$(8:1:b) \qquad x_2 = a_2 p_2 + b_2 p_1 + c_2,$$

where a_1, a_2, b_1, b_2, c_1, and c_2 are constants and a_1 and a_2 are negative quantities. The conjectural variations are given by the following equations:

$$(8:2:a) \qquad \bar{p}_2 = m_1 p_1 + n_1 p_2{}^0,$$

$$(8:2:b) \qquad \bar{p}_1 = m_2 p_2 + n_2 p_1{}^0,$$

where m_1, m_2, n_1, and n_2 are constants, and the other notations are as defined in Secs. 5.5.4 and 5.5.5.

We may rewrite equations (8:1:a and b) as:

$$(8:3:a) \qquad \bar{x}_1 = a_1 p_1 + b_1 \bar{p}_2 + c_1,$$

$$(8:3:b) \qquad \bar{x}_2 = a_2 p_2 + b_2 \bar{p}_1 + c_2,$$

where $\bar{x}_1$ and $\bar{x}_2$ are the amounts that sellers 1 and 2 think they can sell in the next period.

The cost functions are given by,

$$(8:4:a) \qquad c_1(x_1) = \alpha_1 x_1{}^2 + \beta_1 x_1 + \gamma_1,$$

---

[2] Arthur Smithies, "Equilibrium in Monopolistic Competition," *Quarterly Journal of Economics*, LV (1940), p. 95.

[3] Arthur Smithies, "The Stability of Competitive Equilibrium," *Econometrica*, X (1942), p. 248.

(8:4:b) $$c_2(x_2) = \alpha_2 x_2{}^2 + \beta_2 x_2 + \gamma_2$$

where α_1, α_2 β_1, β_2, γ_1, and γ_2 are constants.

Profits are defined as:

(8:5:a) $$g_1 = p_1 \bar{x}_1 - c_1(\bar{x}_1),$$

(8:5:b) $$g_2 = p_2 \bar{x}_2 - c_2(\bar{x}_2).$$

Using the same method of substitution as in Sec. 5.5.4, we can derive g_1 as a function of p_1 and parameter $p_2{}^0$ and g_2 as a function of p_2 and parameter $p_1{}^0$. Then for maximum profits, $\partial g_1/\partial p_1$ and $\partial g_2/\partial p_2$ are equated to zero and they give the following reaction functions:

(8:6:a) $$A_1 p_1 + B_1 p_2{}^0 + C_1 = 0,$$

(8:6:b) $$A_2 p_2 + B_2 p_1{}^0 + C_2 = 0,$$

where A_1, A_2, B_1, B_2, C_1, and C_2 are constants derived from the above manipulations of substitutions and maximization.

Equations (8:6:a and b) can be solved for equilibrium values of $p_1 = p_1{}^0$ and $p_2 = p_2{}^0$.

9. PROFESSOR CHAMBERLIN'S THEORY

9.1. *General outline of the approach and assumptions*

9.1.1. We will consider in this section Professor Chamberlin's "group" problem, namely, the problem of adjustment of prices and "products" of a number of producers whose goods are fairly close substitutes. The "group" is one "which has ordinarily been regarded as composing one imperfectly competitive market: a number of automobile manufacturers, of producers of pots and pans, of magazine publishers, or of retail shoe dealers."[4] The sales of a seller in a group depend on his price and the prices of the others in the group; Professor Chamberlin's definition of "group" is therefore the same as our definition of "market."

9.1.2. In his analysis, Chamberlin makes use of demand and cost curves which have one peculiar feature, namely, "both

---

[4] E. H. Chamberlin, *The Theory of Monopolistic Competition*, 7th edition (Cambridge, Mass.: Harvard University Press, 1956), p. 81.

demand and cost curves for all the products are uniform through-out the group."[5] As we shall see in Sec. 9.2.2, this assumption is made to facilitate graphic representation and solution of the problem. Although the assumption is not explicitly stated by Professor Chamberlin, we may draw inferences from a type of demand curve that he uses in his book, so that we may be able to formulate the symmetry assumption mathematically.

He describes a demand curve dd',[6] which will show the demand for the product of any one seller at various prices when a uniform price is fixed by all other sellers.

(9:1) If the demand curves for seller i ($i = 1, 2, \ldots, n$) are de-rived by assuming $p_1 = p_2 = \cdots = p_{i-1} = p_{i+1} = \cdots p_n = \lambda$, then all these demand curves will be identical.

According to assumption (9:1), we can write the demand functions in the symmetrical form:

(9:2:a) $x_i = h(p_1) + \cdots + f(p_i) + \cdots h(p_n),$

where f and h represent functions, linear or nonlinear.

(9:2:a) may be expressed in a symmetrical matrix form:

$$(9:2:b) \quad \begin{bmatrix} x_1 \\ x_2 \\ x_3 \\ \cdot \\ \cdot \\ \cdot \\ x_n \end{bmatrix} = \begin{bmatrix} f & h & h & \cdots & h \\ h & f & h & \cdots & h \\ h & h & f & \cdots & h \\ \cdot & \cdot & \cdot & \cdots & \cdot \\ \cdot & \cdot & \cdot & \cdots & \cdot \\ \cdot & \cdot & \cdot & \cdots & \cdot \\ h & h & h & \cdots & f \end{bmatrix} \begin{bmatrix} p_1 \\ p_2 \\ p_3 \\ \cdot \\ \cdot \\ \cdot \\ p_n \end{bmatrix}.$$

9.1.3. Professor Chamberlin's analysis allows for a market with free exit and free entry of sellers. Under these conditions, new firms would enter into a group when AR (average revenue) exceeds AC (average cost including normal profits), and old firms would drop out when AC exceeds AR; hence in equilibrium $AR = AC$.

9.1.4. Professor Chamberlin uses two fundamental cases:

[5] Chamberlin, *Monopolistic Competition*, p. 82.
[6] Chamberlin, *Monopolistic Competition*, p. 90.

(9:A) group solution with a large number of sellers,[7] and

(9:B) group solution with a small number of sellers.

9.2. *The case of a large number of sellers*

9.2.1. Assuming the cost function, which is identical for every seller, to be a function c of his own quantity, we have the following profit equations for the sellers:

$$(9:3) \qquad g_i = p_i x_i(p_1, p_2, \ldots, p_n) - c(x_i).$$

For maximum profits,

$$\frac{\partial g_i}{\partial p_j} = 0. \qquad (j = 1, 2, \ldots, n)$$

For $i \neq j$,

$$\frac{\partial g_i}{\partial p_j} = x_i(p_1, \ldots, p_n) \frac{\partial p_i}{\partial p_j} + p_i \frac{\partial x_i}{\partial p_j} - \frac{\partial c}{\partial p_j}.$$

Because of the assumption that there are a large number of sellers,

a) $$\frac{\partial p_i}{\partial p_j} \equiv 0,$$

and from equation (5:6)

b) $$p_i \frac{\partial x_i}{\partial p_j} \equiv 0,$$

c) $$\frac{\partial c}{\partial p_j} \equiv 0,$$

because it is given that c does not vary with p_j. Hence $\partial g_i / \partial p_j$, when $i \neq j$, is identically equal to zero.

Therefore, for any seller i, there is only one condition for maximum profits, namely,

$$\frac{\partial g_i}{\partial p_i} = 0.$$

Writing this out for all the sellers and using the demand equations of (9:2), we have the following system of equations:

[7] For the criticism of this type of solution, see Secs. 5.3.5 and 5.3.6.

$$\frac{\partial g_1}{\partial p_1} = f(p_1) + p_1 \frac{\partial f}{\partial p_1} + h(p_2)$$

$$+ h(p_3) + \cdots + h(p_n) \qquad -\frac{\partial c}{\partial p_1} = 0,$$

$$\frac{\partial g_2}{\partial p_2} = h(p_1) \qquad + f(p_2) + p_2 \frac{\partial f}{\partial p_2}$$

$$+ h(p_3) + \cdots + h(p_n) \qquad -\frac{\partial c}{\partial p_2} = 0,$$

(9:4) $\cdots$ . . . .

$$\frac{\partial g_n}{\partial p_n} = h(p_1) \qquad + h(p_2)$$

$$+ h(p_3) + \cdots + f(p_n) + p_n \frac{\partial f}{\partial p_n} - \frac{\partial c}{\partial p_n} = 0.$$

(9:C) One of the solutions of this system of equations is

$$p_1 = p_2, \ldots, p_n = \alpha,$$

where $\quad f(\alpha) + \alpha \dfrac{\partial f}{\partial p_{(\alpha)}} + h(\alpha)(n-1) - \dfrac{\partial c}{\partial p_{(\alpha)}} = 0.$[8]

Because of the assumption of "free entry," as mentioned in 9.1.3., the additional condition that (9:3) be equal to 0 must also be satisfied for a complete solution.

9.2.2. To depict the above equilibrium position graphically, Chamberlin needs only three curves, as shown in Fig. 4: the first curve is DD', "which shows the demand for the product of any one seller at various prices on the assumption that his competitors' prices are always identical with his."[9] The second curve is

---

[8] $\dfrac{\partial f}{\partial p_{(\alpha)}}, \dfrac{\partial c}{\partial p_{(\alpha)}}$ represent the derivatives of f and c, with respect to p, at the point $p = \alpha$.

[9] Chamberlin, *Monopolistic Competition*, p. 90. In terms of the demand functions of (9:2), DD' curve will take the functional form: $x = f(a) + (n-1)h(a)$, where a is a parameter. This figure is reproduced from Fig. 14 of Chamberlin's *Theory of Monopolistic Competition* with the permission of The Harvard University Press.

the dd'[10] already described in Sec. 9.1.2. The third curve is PP', the average cost curve. Graphically, the complete solution in Sec. 9.1.2 means that the point which gives the equilibrium price and output in Fig. 4 is at R, where dd' is tangent to PP', and DD' passes through R.

Professor Chamberlin approaches the equilibrium position in the following way: He chooses a point Q on curve DD' as an initial position, thus assuming that all sellers are charging the same price at the initial position. Each seller then assumes that

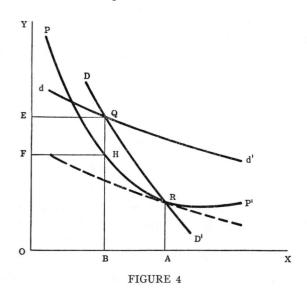

FIGURE 4

the other sellers are holding their prices fast at BQ; hence the demand curve facing each seller is represented by a dd' curve drawn through Q. To maximize his profits, each seller would then move to the right along dd' until the marginal revenue of the dd' curve equals the marginal cost. As all the sellers have identical dd' and cost curves, every seller would select the same new price, and at this new price level, no one will sell the amount

[10] The dd' curve will take the functional form: $x = f(p) + (n-1)h(a)$, where p is a variable and a a parameter.

represented by dd' but rather the actual sales will be shown by the curve DD'. As the same type of movement takes place subsequently, the approach to equilibrium is depicted by the dd' curve sliding downwards along the DD' curve as prices are lowered, and the movement comes to a stop at the price AR.

9.2.3. In the graphic presentation of solution (9:C), we see that there are an infinite number of approaches to the equilibrium position and that if it is to be assumed that at the initial position all prices are not equal, the equilibrium position will be different.

9.2.4. It should be noted that although Professor Chamberlin arrives at (9:C) as the solution to (9:4), it is just one of the solutions possible. As shown below, (9:C) is the unique solution of (9:4) only if the demand and cost functions are linear and if the demand functions in (9:2) take the form given in (9:5).[11]

$$
\begin{aligned}
(9:5) \quad
x_1 &= -ap_1 + bp_2 + bp_3 \cdots + bp_n + k, \\
x_2 &= bp_1 - ap_2 + bp_3 \cdots + bp_n + k, \\
&\cdot \quad \cdot \quad \cdot \quad \cdot \quad \cdot \quad \cdot \\
x_n &= bp_1 + bp_2 + bp_3 \cdots - ap_n + k.
\end{aligned}
$$

If the cost functions are given simply as a proportion c of the quantity, we have the following profit equations:

$$
\begin{aligned}
(9:6) \quad
g_1 &= -ap_1^2 + bp_1p_2 + bp_1p_3 + \cdots + bp_1p_n + kp_1 - cx_1, \\
g_2 &= bp_2p_1 - ap_2^2 + bp_2p_3 + \cdots + bp_2p_n + kp_2 - cx_2, \\
&\cdot \quad \cdot \quad \cdot \quad \cdot \quad \cdot \quad \cdot \quad \cdot \\
g_n &= bp_np_1 + bp_np_2 + bp_np_3 + \cdots - ap_n^2 + kp_n - cx_n.
\end{aligned}
$$

For maximum profits, $\partial g_i / \partial p_i = 0$, $i = 1, 2, \ldots, n$, and from (9:6), it means

$$
\begin{aligned}
(9:7) \quad
2ap_1 &- bp_2 - bp_3 - \cdots - bp_n = k + ac,^{12} \\
-bp_1 &+ 2ap_2 - bp_3 - \cdots - bp_n = k + ac, \\
&\cdot \quad \cdot \quad \cdot \quad \cdot \quad \cdot \quad \cdot \quad \cdot \\
-bp_1 &- bp_2 - bp_3 \cdots + 2ap_n = k + ac.
\end{aligned}
$$

Taking any two sellers, say for convenience 1 and 2, we have the following solutions from (9:7):

---

[11] To simplify the problem, the condition in which $AR = AC$ is not included in the solution.

[12] $(\partial/\partial p_i)cx_i = c(\partial x_i/\partial p_i)$, but from (9:5) $\partial x_i/\partial p_i = -a$; hence $(\partial/\partial p_i)cx_i = -ac$.

(9:8)
$$p_1 = \frac{\begin{vmatrix} k+ac & -b & -b & \cdots & -b \\ k+ac & 2a & -b & \cdots & -b \\ \cdot & \cdot & \cdot & \cdots & \cdot \\ \cdot & \cdot & \cdot & \cdots & \cdot \\ \cdot & \cdot & \cdot & \cdots & \cdot \\ k+ac & -b & -b & \cdots & 2a \end{vmatrix}}{|D|}$$

(9:9)
$$p_2 = \frac{\begin{vmatrix} 2a & k+ac & -b & \cdots & -b \\ -b & k+ac & -b & \cdots & -b \\ \cdot & \cdot & \cdot & \cdots & \cdot \\ \cdot & \cdot & \cdot & \cdots & \cdot \\ \cdot & \cdot & \cdot & \cdots & \cdot \\ -b & k+ac & -b & \cdots & 2a \end{vmatrix}}{|D|}$$

where
$$D = \begin{vmatrix} 2a & -b & -b & \cdots & -b \\ -b & 2a & -b & \cdots & -b \\ \cdot & \cdot & \cdot & \cdots & \cdot \\ \cdot & \cdot & \cdot & \cdots & \cdot \\ \cdot & \cdot & \cdot & \cdots & \cdot \\ -b & -b & -b & \cdots & 2a \end{vmatrix}.$$

If we interchange the first and second rows and also inter-change the first and second columns in the numerator of (9:9), (9:8) and (9:9) are then identical. From the theorem of deter-minants, we know that an interchange of any two rows *or* of any two columns of a determinant will merely change the sign of the determinant, and that when we interchange the two rows *as well as* the two columns, the sign of the determinant will re-main unchanged. Hence the transposed (9:9) will be the same as the original (9:8) so that $p_1 = p_2$. Similarly we can show that in equilibrium $p_1 = p_2 = p_3 = \cdots = p_n$.

9.3. *The case of a small number of sellers*

9.3.1. In the case of the small group, three types of solu-tions are given: in the first type the sellers assume that their rivals' prices are fixed, in the second type the sellers assume that their rivals' quantities are fixed, and in the third type each seller seeks "to maximize his profit with regard for his full influence, direct and indirect, upon the situation."[13]

The solution of the first type is identical with that of the case of a large number of sellers for a given demand function and a cost function. In the first type, a seller, say i, would assume the rivals' prices to be fixed; in other words the subsidiary condition for the seller i in maximizing his profits is that $p_j = \bar{p}_j$,[14] or, the same thing, partial derivatives $\partial g_i/\partial p_j$, $i \neq j$, would be supposed to be identically equal to zero, and for i we are left with only one equation, $\partial g_i/\partial p_i = 0$. Though not for the same reason, as in the case of the large number of sellers, we do the same thing to maximize profits, that is, we make $\partial g_i/\partial p_i$ equal to 0.

9.3.2. Professor Chamberlin also has a definite solution for the second type, though he does not show how it is derived. For this type of problem, demand functions must be expressed with quantities x_i as independent variables, in which case we then solve the problem by maximizing profits with respect to x_i.

9.3.3. The third type is the most interesting one though dealt with only briefly by Professor Chamberlin. His solution is a point on the DD' curve where the profits to a seller as given by the DD' curve are maximum. He describes this point as the price "yielding the maximum total profits to all,"[15] and according to him, this price is the stable equilibrium price, because "any individual could, by reducing his price from this point, secure the larger profits indicated by the demand curve dd', *provided* the others did not follow suit. But since their own losses by his action would be considerable, the proviso does not hold. Each would, therefore, hold his price at BQ because the *ultimate* consequences of his doing anything else would be less advantageous."[16]

This solution is designated by Professor Chamberlin as the "mutual dependence recognised" solution. This treatment of the problem marks the turning point in the whole literature on oligopoly. The following passage from one of the recent writings

[13] Chamberlin, *Monopolistic Competition*, p. 100.
[14] Here $\bar{p}_i$ is a parameter.
[15] Chamberlin, *Monopolistic Competition*, p. 100.
[16] Chamberlin, *Monopolistic Competition*, pp. 100–101.

of Professor Chamberlin gives the reader a concise historical development of the theory of oligopoly and also gives the core of this "mutual dependence recognised" solution:

A feature of "duopoly" theory in the mid-twenties was that it ignored almost entirely the "mutual dependence recognised" solutions — that phase of the subject which is now thought by many to be the essence, or even the very definition, of the oligopoly problem. Such recognition is, of course, foreign to both the Cournot and Edgeworth solutions, which, as has been pointed out above, dominated the scene. Irving Fisher, advancing the game analogy (chess) for the first time to my knowledge (1898), and H. L. Moore (1906) had both criticised Cournot on this score, but neither one carried the matter further. Pigou (1924) again presented the chess analogy, but seemed to think that it led to Edgeworthian oscillation (although proposing a new set of limits which has always been completely mysterious to me); and three years later (1927) Wicksell, arguing also for the recognition of mutual dependence, rejected Edgeworth *because* he had ignored it, and favoured Cournot (who had equally ignored it!). To me at that time, the real problem seemed to be to develop "mutual dependence recognised" as a separate category, and to make clear that it had nothing to do with either Cournot or Edgeworth, both of whom had, on the contrary, assumed that mutual dependence was ignored.

I take this opportunity finally to comment on a phase of the "mutual dependence recognised" category, which has become so important in the recent development of the theory. The solutions under this heading in my own case were multifarious, involving time lags, frictions and a variety of uncertainties. They all took, however, as their point of departure, a conception of the fundamental nature of the problem which has been much misunderstood, and has even been rejected as "incorrect" by Stackelberg. It involves the distinction between (1) the *direct* effect which a seller has upon price and (2) the *indirect* effect, which includes the moves his rival makes *as a consequence of his own;* and holds that for a seller to take the second as well as the first into account is fully consistent with *independent* action. Although the solution if *each* seller thus takes account of his *total* influence on the price may be the same in terms of prices, outputs and profits as if there were an agreement, there are excellent reasons for making clear that no agreement is involved — not even "tacit" agreement, quasi-agreement or "spontaneous co-operation." In other words, this is a *legitimate* solution of *oligopoly*, consistent with complete independence of the sellers, and not to be excluded on the false ground that there is an agreement in *some* sense, and hence monopoly.

In defence of this view, an appeal to the analogy of chess may be useful. Clearly if a chess player decides against a particular move because the responses to it which his rival would make would be damaging to him, he cannot be accused of "spontaneous co-operation": and he should hardly be *required* by the rules to make the move on the ground that otherwise he would be entering into a "conspiracy in restraint of chess," or into an agreement with his rival. Why, then, should a business-man who acts with equal (and rather ordinary) intelligence in deciding not to make a price cut, be accused (either by economists or by Attorneys General) of "collusion," or of *tacitly* "co-operating" with someone? The point is that the idea of "co-operation" in *any* sense is *unnecessary* to the result. [To which, Chamberlin adds the footnote:] Of course, agreements, both actual and tacit, are extremely common in reality, and there is certainly no intention to deny them where they are in fact present.[17]

Here too it should be noted that Chamberlin's solution is only one of a number of possible solutions. He arrives at this particular one because of the nature of the initial position, which happens to be a point on the DD' curve. The question is, why should the sellers choose the DD' curve as their line of approach? An obvious reason is that all the sellers have made some kind of tacit agreement that everyone will have an equal share of the profits. Only then could we say that the solution given by Professor Chamberlin is the only solution which will yield "the maximum total profits to all."

The same type of criticism can also be made of Chamberlin's solution of Cournot's type of market. Chamberlin's solution is that the two sellers will share equally the output that will bring the monopoly price and profits "because the *ultimate* consequences of his [either seller's] following through the other chain of adjustments are less advantageous to himself than to share equally with his rival . . . The price . . . is perfectly stable, under our assumptions, for either seller would, by departing from it, bring disaster upon *himself* as well as upon his rival."[18]

This criticism is discussed in detail in Chapter VI below. The solution I have offered in Chapters IV and V is a generalized version of Chamberlin's "mutual dependence recognised" solution.

[17] "On the Origin of 'Oligopoly,' " *Economic Journal*, LXVII (June 1957), pp. 215–216.
[18] Chamberlin, *Monopolistic Competition*, p. 47.

10. STACKELBERG'S THEORY

10.1. *General outline of Stackelberg's theory*

10.1.1. Stackelberg advanced the novel idea of a subsidiary condition for maximizing profits.[19] Unlike Chamberlin, Stackelberg does not make use of demand and cost curves in his main analysis, but introduces constant profit curves showing different levels of profit as dependent on different prices or quantities offered in the market. Let us take one of Stackelberg's many examples, that of two sellers with prices as independent variables. The constant profit curves of Stackelberg can be expressed in the following functional form:

$$g_1 = g_1(p_1, p_2),$$
$$g_2 = g_2(p_1, p_2).$$

Stackelberg offers three types of solutions, two of which are of equilibrium form and the third of disequilibrium form. Section 10.1.2 describes the case which gives the "leadership equilibrium" solution; Sec. 10.1.3 describes the case which gives the "followership equilibrium" solution; and Sec. 10.1.4 describes the case which gives the "leadership disequilibrium" solution.

10.1.2. To get the solution of "leadership equilibrium," the sellers are assumed to behave as follows:

(10:A) One seller, say seller 1, would regard the existing price of the other seller, say seller 2, as a datum and maximize his profits accordingly. In other words, seller 1 equates $\partial g_1/\partial p_1$ to zero, assuming $\bar{p}_2 = p_2{}^0$ a parameter.

(10:B) Seller 2, on the other hand, maximizes his profits with the conjecture that seller 1 would behave as in (10:A). In other words, seller 2, in maximizing his profits $g_2(p_1, p_2)$, conjectures that 1 would equate $\partial g_1/\partial p_1$ to zero, assuming $\bar{p}_2 = p_2{}^0$.

As (10:B) contains (10:A), the problem becomes one of maximizing the function $g_2(p_1, p_2)$ with $\partial g_1/\partial p_1$ equal to 0 as a subsidiary condition.

[19] H. von Stackelberg, *Marktform und Gleichgewicht*, Vienna and Berlin, 1934. Professor Fellner gives a lucid description of Stackelberg's case on pp. 98–119.

As the number of subsidiary conditions is less than the number of unknown variables, p_1 and p_2 can be solved. A seller who behaves like seller 1 in (10:A) is called the follower and one who behaves like seller 2 in (10:B) is called the leader. In this case, as p_1 and p_2 can be solved, the case is said to be of an equilibrium type and the name "leadership equilibrium" is given to it.

10.1.3. In the "followership equilibrium" case, let seller 1 behave like seller 1 in (10:A) and let seller 2 also behave in the same way.[20] Both are then said to be followers and both are wrong in their conjectures.[21] But we still have a solution for p_1 and p_2, as we have two equations and two unknowns as follows:

Seller 1 equates $\partial g_1/\partial p_1$ to zero, assuming $\bar{p}_2 = p_2{}^0$, and this gives p_1 as a function of p_2, say $p_1 = R_1(p_2)$, and similarly as seller 2 equates $\partial g_2/\partial p_2$ to zero, assuming $\bar{p}_1 = p_1{}^0$, we have p_2 as a function of p_1, say $p_2 = R_2(p_1)$. Functions R_1 and R_2 are called reaction functions for 1 and 2, respectively, and these two together will give a solution for p_1 and p_2. This type of solution may be called a "followership equilibrium" or "Cournot type equilibrium" solution.

10.1.4. The disequilibrium case is one in which both sellers want to behave as leaders, that is, seller 1 would maximize $g_1(p_1, p_2)$ with the conjecture that 2 would act as a follower, equating $\partial g_2/\partial p_2$ to zero; seller 2 on the other hand would maximize $g_2(p_1, p_2)$ with the conjecture that 1 would act as a follower and equate $\partial g_1/\partial p_1$ to zero.

We will have in this case two sets of solutions for p_1 and p_2, namely, one set of solutions with seller 2 as leader, which will be the same as that of 10.1.2, and the other set of solutions, similarly derived, but with seller 1 as a leader. Let us name these two sets, set I and set II, respectively. In set I, 1 is the follower and 2 is the leader and in set II, 1 is the leader and 2 is the follower. Let us denote the profits of 1 and 2 in the first set by $g_1(I)$ and $g_2(I)$, respectively, and the profits of 1 and 2 in the second set by $g_1(II)$ and $g_2(II)$, respectively.

In the case under discussion, seller 1 is striving to obtain the

[20] This means that seller 2 equates $\partial g_2/\partial p_2$ to zero, assuming $\bar{p}_1 = p_1{}^0$.

[21] In the "leadership equilibrium" type 10.1.2, it is to be noted that seller 2's conjecture is correct.

set II solution and seller 2 is striving to obtain the set I solution; hence there will be a struggle between the two sellers. The solution is therefore a disequilibrium solution.

10.1.5. Stackelberg states that the following conditions[22] will lead the sellers to behave as in 10.1.2, 10.1.3, or 10.1.4.

(10:C) If $g_1(\text{I})$ is greater than $g_1(\text{II})$, and at the same time $g_2(\text{II})$ is greater than $g_2(\text{I})$, both sellers would find followership preferable to leadership and each would adjust to the given value of the other's variable. In other words, seller 1 would equate $\partial g_1/\partial p_1$ to zero and seller 2 would equate $\partial g_2/\partial p_2$ to zero and the result would be the solution given in Sec. 10.1.3.

(10:D) If $g_1(\text{I})$ is greater than $g_1(\text{II})$, and at the same time $g_2(\text{I})$ is greater than $g_2(\text{II})$, both sellers would strive to obtain the solution of set I and the result would be the leadership equilibrium solution described in Sec. 10.1.2.

The same kind of leadership equilibrium will result with seller 1 as a leader, with both sellers striving to obtain the solution of set II, if $g_1(\text{II})$ is greater than $g_1(\text{I})$, and at the same time $g_2(\text{II})$ is greater than $g_2(\text{I})$.

(10:E) Leadership would be preferable to both sellers if $g_1(\text{II})$ is greater than $g_1(\text{I})$, and at the same time $g_2(\text{I})$ is greater than $g_2(\text{II})$. Then both would be striving for leadership and thus for different equilibriums. These conditions will give rise to the situation described in Sec. 10.1.4. "This struggle may last any length of time, or it may end by the submission of one party into followership."[23]

11. PROFESSOR FELLNER'S APPROACH

11.1. *His general assumptions*

11.1. Professor Fellner first recognizes the existence of conjectural interdependence in oligopoly[24] and then goes on to

---

[22] See William Fellner, *Competition among the Few* (New York: Knopf, 1949), p. 100.

[23] Fellner, p. 100.

[24] Fellner, pp. 11–15.

show the relation between conjectural interdependence, bargaining, quasi-bargaining, "true" agreement and quasi-agreement as follows:

> Bargaining in the usual sense presupposes conjectural interdependence, but bargaining in the *usual sense* does not take place in all cases in which conjectural interdependence exists. Bargaining in the usual sense requires direct contact and negotiations between the parties concerned, in addition to conjectural interdependence. But, it will be argued in this volume that there is no fundamental difference between those instances of conjectural interdependence which lead to explicit bargaining and those which do not. In the one case, explicit negotiations are carried on, and, in the course of these, the parties concerned attempt to find out by direct observation what the most favorable agreement is which they can reach with the others. In the other case, each party tries to find out from the responses of the other parties what the ultimate consequences of its own patterns of behavior are; and each party tries to discover which of the alternative patterns of behavior results in mutual reactions that are in the nature of a tacit agreement (or convention), and are more favorable from his point of view than any other tacit agreement acceptable to the others. Such processes may be termed implicit bargaining or quasi-bargaining and the resulting state of affairs may be termed quasi-agreement. The difference between "true" agreement and quasi-agreement is that the former requires direct contact while the latter does not . . . We may say that all problems of conjectural interdependence are essentially problems of bargaining — provided we interpret bargaining in the broader sense, including the "implicit" variety, that is, quasi-bargaining.[25]

Further on, Fellner expresses the main suggestions of his book:

> In markets of the oligopolistic . . . kind, *there is a tendency toward the maximization of the joint profits of the group and toward division of these profits* . . . This proposition follows directly from the assumption (and from the observed fact) that bargaining "normally" leads to an agreement. When it does, the parties will surely not be indifferent to the size of the pie they are now dividing. Jointly they have the size of the pie under control.[26]

Thus, in Professor Fellner's view, conjectural interdependence will be present in oligopoly, but this will lead to quasi-bargaining, which will again lead to quasi-agreement. Quasi-agreement will take the form of division of the profits (without transfer) with the result that joint-profits will be maximized. This is the crux of Professor Fellner's theory, as we shall see in the next section.

[25] Fellner, pp. 15–16.
[26] Fellner, p. 33, italics mine.

11.2. *Mathematical solution in the case of two sellers*[27]

Let the profits of the two sellers be represented by the following functions:

(11:1:a) $$g_1 = g_1(p_1, p_2),$$

(11:1:b) $$g_2 = g_2(p_1, p_2).$$

Let us assume that sellers 1 and 2 have reached a quasi-agreement to share the profits in the proportion of $\alpha:1-\alpha$; that is, if γ is the joint-profits,

(11:2:a) $$\alpha\gamma = g_1(p_1, p_2),$$

(11:2:b) $$(1 - \alpha)\gamma = g_2(p_1, p_2).$$

For a given value of γ, the left hand sides of equations (11:2:a and b) are constants and the equations can be solved for p_1 and p_2. By varying the value of γ, we obtain various sets of values for p_1 and p_2; and assuming them to be continuous, we can express p_1 as a function of p_2, say $p_1 = \theta(p_2)$, and the values of p_1 and p_2 of this function will satisfy, for given values of γ, equations (11:2:a and b).

Substituting p_1 as given by the θ function for p_2 in equation (11:1:a) we have g_1 expressed as a function of p_1 alone as a variable, and g_1 will be maximum when $\partial g_1/\partial p_1 = 0$. Then equilibrium prices p_1 and p_2 will be obtained and by the subsidiary condition given by the θ-function, g_2 will be maximum at these prices.

12. JOAN ROBINSON'S THEORY

12.1. *The two problems in the market with imperfect competition*

Before we discuss Joan Robinson's theory, we should note that the theories we have already discussed deal with two problems, the main one being economic and the subsidiary one mathematical. The economic problem is to make a careful study of a

---

[27] Professor Fellner gives a graphic solution for the case of equal shares on pp. 200–201, using demand and cost functions, and on p. 237, a graphic solution is given using the Stackelberg map, that is, the map that represents equations (11:1:a and b) graphically.

market and then make an assumption with regard to how each seller would conjecture the level of other sellers' prices. After having done that, the $n - 1$ unknowns facing each seller become assumed parameters and each seller is thus left with a demand function with only his price or his quantity as a variable. The mathematical problem then has to be considered, and this is a straightforward one of maximizing each seller's profits by using the demand function described above and the given cost conditions. The result is that each seller equates his marginal revenue to his marginal costs.

12.2. *The one problem Joan Robinson treats*

12.2. The core of the problem in a market with imperfect competition is the study of the conjectures of the individual seller as to how other sellers would fix their prices or quantities, or, what is the same thing, it is the study of how an individual seller would select a demand function, with only his price or his quantity as a variable, from all the possible combinations. It is to be regretted that Joan Robinson does not treat this problem in her book, *The Economics of Imperfect Competition*. Instead, she uses a type of individual demand curve which takes into account the effect of price changes of other sellers and which is therefore similar to the reaction curve.[28] She devotes her discussion to the one remaining problem, that is, the mathematical one of maximizing profits.

[28] See Joan Robinson, *The Economics of Imperfect Competition* (London: Macmillan, 1933), p. 21. This deficiency in her book was later admitted by Mrs. Robinson in her article "Imperfect Competition Revisited," *Economic Journal*, LXIII (September 1953), p. 584, section 3.

CHAPTER IV

Rational Pricing in a Market with Two Sellers

13. THE SIMPLE MARKET WITH TWO SELLERS

13.1. *Formulation of the approach*

13.1.1. The procedure that we intend to follow can at this point be described. This will be done by first giving an outline of the procedure and then by giving a detailed account of the main concepts and devices involved.

In developing a theory of the behavior of sellers, we should consider both the motive of each seller and the rules which tell him how to behave in every conceivable situation so as to attain his objectives.

13.1.2. The motives of a seller may be one of the following two types:

(A) to obtain as much profit as possible for himself, irrespective of whether this action would make the rival sellers better or worse off, or

(B) to wage a price war so that rival sellers would incur losses and finally be forced out of competition, even if by so doing his profits suffer a temporary setback.

In this work we assume that sellers have motive (A) in deciding their actions, unless otherwise stated.

13.1.3. Our main concern in this section is with the second problem, namely, determining how each seller would behave to attain his objectives once they are decided upon.

13.1.4. We have seen in previous chapters how various authors, in describing the behavior of sellers in an imperfectly competitive market, assume that the sellers first conjecture what the rival sellers will do and then act either independently or by some tacit agreement amongst some or all of the sellers.

The solution of these authors depends on the type of conjectures that the sellers are assumed to make. But the *nature* of the conjectures that are prescribed or described for the sellers by these various authors does not vary in accordance with all possible profit and price situations in the market. Because of this restriction, although equilibrium situations are attained at certain profits and prices, there are still some regions where the profits for all the sellers are higher than those attained in the equilibrium positions.

In such situations, the behavior of the sellers cannot be said to be "rational."

We shall now approach the problem in a different way. To get the rational behavior we will assume that sellers do not have just one fixed conjecture for all situations, but that they change their conjecture according to the kind of situation they are faced with. This approach may be stated as follows:

Suppose that g_1^0 and g_2^0 represent the profits of sellers 1 and 2 in a particular situation, and that g_1' and g_2' represent the profits of these two sellers in the next situation; then in the neighborhood of the original situation there may exist regions in which

$$(13:A) \qquad g_1' < g_1^0 \quad \text{and} \quad g_2' > g_2^0,$$

$$(13:B) \qquad g_1' > g_1^0 \quad \text{and} \quad g_2' > g_2^0,$$

$$(13:C) \qquad g_1' > g_1^0 \quad \text{and} \quad g_2' < g_2^0,$$

$$(13:D) \qquad g_1' < g_1^0 \quad \text{and} \quad g_2' < g_2^0.$$

Our task is to find out what types of motives, conjectures, and behaviors would move the sellers in or out of these different regions, and further to determine whether it is plausible to assume that our sellers would adopt such motives, conjectures, or behaviors in such situations.

13.2. *Setting up the tools for the analysis*

13.2.1. We shall make a number of simplifying assumptions. There are two sellers in our market, selling a differentiated product. The goods are produced at the lowest possible cost and a certain profit mark-up is added to this basic cost. The adjustment to obtain maximum profit is made by varying this profit mark-up,[1] the quality of the product and the advertising costs being kept constant.

Let us denote the two sellers by 1 and 2, their prices by p_1 and p_2, respectively, and their profits by g_1 and g_2, respectively. Profits g_1 and g_2 each depend on prices p_1 and p_2:

(13:1:a) $$g_1 = g_1(p_1, p_2),$$

(13:1:b) $$g_2 = g_2(p_1, p_2).$$

13.2.2. We will now take up the simplest of the markets in each of which, throughout the price ranges considered, the derivatives $\partial g_1/\partial p_1$, $\partial g_1/\partial p_2$, $\partial g_2/\partial p_1$ and $\partial g_2/\partial p_2$ are assumed not to change their signs with the change in the prices p_1 and p_2. The implications of this assumption are shown below.

Suppose p_2 is kept constant at a certain level, then seller 1's sales would be a function of p_1 alone, that is, the demand function facing seller 1 would be $x_1 = x_1(p_1)$, or in the inverse form $p_1 = p_1(x_1)$.

The demand and cost curves are assumed to be of the form shown in Fig. 5, where dd' is the demand, mr the marginal revenue, and mc the marginal cost curve. As p_1 increases, the profits first increase and then reach maximum at output OA, where $mr = mc$, and then decrease again. For an output less than OA, $\partial g_1/\partial x_1 > 0$; we will name this region the β region. For those outputs greater than the output at which profit is maximum, $\partial g_1/\partial x_1 < 0$; we will name this region the α region.

Such α and β regions can also be formed for seller 2. To distinguish between the regions of the two sellers, we will use the notations α_1 and β_1 for 1 and α_2 and β_2 for 2.

(13:E) Thus we have for region β_i, $\dfrac{\partial g_i}{\partial x_i} > 0$ and $\dfrac{\partial g_i}{\partial p_i} < 0$,

---

[1] This method of pricing is called "full-cost pricing" or "cost-plus pricing." See R. L. Hall and C. J. Hitch, "Price Theory and Business Behaviour," *Oxford Economic Papers*, No. 2, 1939; see also Joel Dean, *Managerial Economics* (New York: Prentice-Hall, 1951), pp. 444 ff.

and　　　　　　　for region α_i, $\dfrac{\partial g_i}{\partial x_i} < 0$　and　$\dfrac{\partial g_i}{\partial p_i} > 0$.[2]

In an ordinary market, both region α and region β exist for sellers 1 and 2; whether they are in region α or β depends on p_1 and p_2. But here in our special simplified market, it is assumed that there is only one region for each seller, α or β, in the whole market. This not only simplifies the decisions that the sellers have to make but also brings out the peculiarities of these regions, knowledge of which will be useful when we drop this

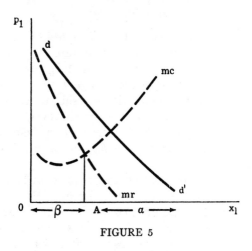

FIGURE 5

simplified assumption and study the ordinary market where both regions α and β exist for each seller.

13.2.3. We will study the behavior of sellers by means of graphic representations accompanied by proofs using elementary differential calculus. Described below are the types of graphs that will be used for this analysis.

In the first case the initial prices are p_1 and p_2, denoted by 1.o and 2.o, respectively. Three possibilities are open to each seller: to keep the price at the old level, to lower the price, or to raise it.

---

[2] Proof: $g_i = \phi(x_i) = \phi[x_i(p_i)]$; $\dfrac{\partial g_i}{\partial p_i} = \dfrac{\partial g_i}{\partial x_i} \cdot \dfrac{\partial x_i}{\partial p_i}$. Since $\partial x_i/\partial p_i$ is negative, $\partial g_i/\partial p_i$ and $\partial g_i/\partial x_i$ assume opposite signs.

If we denote the alternative prices for seller 1 by 1.a and 1.b and for seller 2 by 2.a and 2.b, one of the two prices 1.a and 1.b is less than the initial price 1.o; similarly, for seller 2, either 2.a or 2.b is less than 2.o. The values of $g_1(p_1, p_2)$ and $g_2(p_1, p_2)$ corresponding to the three alternative price levels of p_1 and p_2 can be arranged in a rectangular scheme as in Fig. 6.

Figure 6 is a rectangle of 3 rows and 3 columns, in which p_1 equal to 1.a, 1.o, 1.b designates the rows and p_2 equal to 2.a, 2.o, 2.b designates the columns. In the field of p_1 and p_2, we write the two values of $g_1(p_1, p_2)$ and $g_2(p_1, p_2)$.

	2. a	2. o	2. b
1. a	$g_1(1.\,a, 2.\,a)$ $g_2(1.\,a, 2.\,a)$	$g_1(1.\,a, 2.\,o)$ $g_2(1.\,a, 2.\,o)$	$g_1(1.\,a, 2.\,b)$ $g_2(1.\,a, 2.\,b)$
1. o	$g_1(1.\,o, 2.\,a)$ $g_2(1.\,o, 2.\,a)$	$g_1(1.\,o, 2.\,o)$ $g_2(1.\,o, 2.\,o)$	$g_1(1.\,o, 2.\,b)$ $g_2(1.\,o, 2.\,b)$
1. b	$g_1(1.\,b, 2.\,a)$ $g_2(1.\,b, 2.\,a)$	$g_1(1.\,b, 2.\,o)$ $g_2(1.\,b, 2.\,o)$	$g_1(1.\,b, 2.\,b)$ $g_2(1.\,b, 2.\,b)$

FIGURE 6

Figure 6 may be separated into two rectangular matrices, one with $g_1(p_1, p_2)$ and the other with $g_2(p_1, p_2)$ as matrix elements. For the present, we will assume that the sellers know the values of the matrix elements $g_1(p_1, p_2)$ and $g_2(p_1, p_2)$ of Fig. 6. Let us then take as an example the numerical values given in Fig. 7.

The upper figure in each cell represents g_1 and the lower, g_2; e.g., at the initial prices 1.o and 2.o, seller 1's profits are 80 and seller 2's profits are 90.

The profit figures in Fig. 7 are in keeping with our assumption that the derivatives $\partial g_1/\partial p_1$, $\partial g_1/\partial p_2$, $\partial g_2/\partial p_1$ and $\partial g_2/\partial p_2$ do not change their signs throughout the price ranges in the market. The proof follows.

In Fig. 7, the profit figures for the first seller in row 1.a are less than those in row 1.o in all the columns, that is, $75 < 90$, $70 < 80$, $60 < 70$. We describe this phenomenon by saying: "Seller 1's profits in row 1.o majorize those in 1.a." Further, we find that for seller 1's profits, row 1.b majorizes 1.o, column 2.o majorizes 2.b, and column 2.a majorizes 2.o. Looking at seller 2's profits, we find that row 1.o majorizes 1.a, and 1.b majorizes 1.o; column 2.o majorizes 2.a, and 2.b majorizes 2.o.

Suppose $1.b > 1.o > 1.a$ and $2.b < 2.o < 2.a$. The fact that row 1.o majorizes 1.a and that row 1.b majorizes 1.o means that

	2. a	2. o	2. b
1. a	75 70	70 80	60 85
1. o	90 80	80 90	70 95
1. b	100 90	90 100	80 110

FIGURE 7

when seller 2's price is kept constant at 2.a or 2.o or 2.b, seller 1's profits increase when he increases his price from 1.a to 1.o and from 1.o to 1.b. In other words, $\partial g_1/\partial p_1 > 0$.

Again looking at seller 1's profits, column 2.o majorizes 2.b, and 2.a majorizes 2.o, meaning that when seller 1's price is kept constant at 1.a or 1.o or 1.b, the profits of 1 increase when seller 2 increases his price from 2.b to 2.o and from 2.o to 2.a. In other words, $\partial g_1/\partial p_2 > 0$.

Similarly, for the profits of seller 2, row 1.b majorizes 1.o, and 1.o majorizes 1.a, meaning that $\partial g_2/\partial p_1 > 0$; since column 2.o majorizes 2.a, and 2.b majorizes 2.o, $\partial g_2/\partial p_2 < 0$.

13.2.4. Figure 8 is a graphic representation of the relations shown in Fig. 7. In Fig. 8, g_1 is measured on the horizontal and g_2 on the vertical axis. The values of g_1 and g_2 in each cell of our rectangular matrix of Fig. 7 will now be used as coordinates to plot the points in Fig. 8. First take row 1.o of Fig. 7: the three cells in that row will give us three points with coordinates 90, 80; 80, 90; and 70, 95. We join these points with a curve and designate this curve 1.o. Similarly for rows 1.a and 1.b, we have two curves. We will call these curves constant price curves.[3] By join-

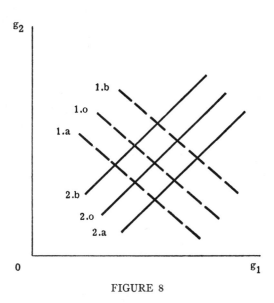

FIGURE 8

ing the points given by the values of g_1 and g_2 of the cells in columns 2.a, 2.o, and 2.b of Fig. 7, we get three curves[4] for seller 2 and we designate these 2.a, 2.o, and 2.b.

In Fig. 8 we find that the constant price curves for 2 rise (from left to right) throughout the interval and those for 1 fall (from

[3] These curves can be represented by the equation $F_1(g_1, g_2) = p_1$, where F_1 represents some functional relationship, p_1 is a parameter, and a family of curves is derived by assigning different values to p_1.

[4] As in the preceding footnote, the family of curves is given by $F_2(g_1, g_2) = p_2$, where p_2 is a parameter. Note that the functions F_1 and F_2 are the inverse functions of g_1 and g_2.

left to right) throughout the interval. Thus for the constant price curves for p_1, an increase in the value of g_1 always causes a decrease in the value of g_2 and the curves are therefore called *monotonic decreasing* curves, while for the constant price curves for p_2, an increase in g_1 always causes an increase in g_2 and the curves are therefore called *monotonic increasing* curves. If the curves have their derivatives dg_2/dg_1 positive everywhere, we have monotonic increasing curves; if the derivatives dg_2/dg_1 are negative everywhere, we have monotonic decreasing curves.

The relationship[5] between $(dg_2/dg_1)_{p_1}$, $(dg_2/dg_1)_{p_2}$, and $\partial g_1/\partial p_1$, $\partial g_1/\partial p_2$, $\partial g_2/\partial p_1$, $\partial g_2/\partial p_2$ is shown in Appendix C.

13.3. *The first case*

13.3.1. We will take Fig. 9 as our first case. The set of broken curves "belongs to" seller 1 and the set of continuous curves "belongs to" seller 2. The words "belongs to" are used in the sense that at any time each seller can only choose one of the curves from the set belonging to him. When both have chosen their respective curves, the values of g_1 and g_2 at the

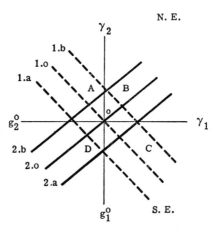

FIGURE 9

[5] $(dg_2/dg_1)_{p_1}$ represents the slope of the constant price curve of p_1 and $(dg_2/dg_1)_{p_2}$ represents the slope of the constant price curve of p_2.

intersection point of the two curves give the share of the profits enjoyed by seller 1 and seller 2, respectively. The curves at the initial position are given by 1.o for seller 1 and by 2.o for seller 2. Point O is the intersection point of the two curves 1.o and 2.o. Let us now shift the origin to this point o, with $g_1{}^0O\gamma_2$ and $g_2{}^0O\gamma_1$ as the new vertical and horizontal axes, respectively. These two axes divide the figure into four quadrants A, B, C, and D, and the properties of these regions are as classified in (13:A to D). In order to get better profits, seller 1 will have to move to region B or region C, and seller 2 to A or B. Thus region B is good and region D is bad for both sellers.

13.3.2. If we look at the situation facing seller 1, we find that whether 2 stays at 2.o or moves to 2.a or 2.b, the best thing for seller 1 to do is to move to 1.b, that is, in a northeasterly direction. Whether 1 stays at 1.o or shifts to 1.a or 1.b, the best thing that seller 2 can do is to move to 2.b, that is, in a northwesterly direction.

13.3.3. We may note here that in this case, seller 2 is in an advantageous position because any action taken by 1 to increase his own profits increases seller 2's profits as well, whereas any action taken by seller 2 to increase g_2 reduces the profits of the other seller.

We can state the result in 13.3.2 as follows:

(13:F) In this market, there is only *one best* course for any seller to follow, no matter how he conjectures the other seller will behave.

13.3.4. To see whether the above statement is true, let us build into our model two types of conjectural variations, those of Cournot and Stackelberg, and find out whether either of these will change the result of Sec. 13.3.2. According to Cournot, one seller assumes that the other seller will keep his price constant. Then from Fig. 9, if seller 1 assumes 2 will keep his price at 2.o, he will move his position to 1.b in order to increase his profits. Similarly, if seller 2 assumes that 1 will keep his price fixed at 1.o, he will now charge the price of 2.b so as to increase his profits. Thus, with Cournot's assumptions, we still have the result of Sec. 13.3.2.

13.3.5. The assumptions for Stackelberg's conjectural variation may be stated as follows: We will consider two markets.[6] First, a market M_1, where seller 1 has to make his choice of p_1 before seller 2 makes his choice of p_2 and where seller 2 makes his choice with a full knowledge of the value given by seller 1 to p_1; and next, a market M_2, which is in all respects like M_1, except that now seller 2 has to make his choice of p_2 before seller 1 makes his choice of p_1, and where 1 makes his choice with a full knowledge of the value given by 2 to p_2.

Let us first consider market M_1. We will assume that in market M_1, seller 1 would conjecture that after he has chosen p_1, seller 2 would choose p_2 so as to make the value of g_2 a maximum for the p_1 chosen by 1. Hence when seller 1 chooses a particular value of p_1, he can foresee what the value of p_2 will be. Now seller 1 wishes to maximize g_1, and hence the best strategy for him is to choose a value of p_1 so that seller 2's choice of p_2 to maximize g_2 would in turn maximize g_1.

Under these conditions, in the case of Fig. 9, seller 1 would choose 1.b and he would assume seller 2 will choose 2.b.

Market M_2 differs from M_1 only in that the roles of sellers 1 and 2 are interchanged. Seller 2 makes his choice of p_2 first and in doing so he conjectures that 1 would choose p_1 to maximize g_1 for the value of p_2 chosen by 2. Hence the best strategy for 2 is to choose p_2 so that 1's choice of p_1 to maximize g_1 would in turn maximize g_2.

Again looking at Fig. 9, seller 2 would choose 2.b and he would assume 1 will choose 1.b. In this case both M_1 and M_2 give the same result, which is also the same as the result derived in Sec. 13.3.2.

13.3.6. We have seen in the above passages how sellers 1 and 2 will behave if their motive is to maximize their profits. Let us now see how they would behave if their motive were to drive one another out of existence. We shall assume first that there are other p_1 and p_2 curves that are not shown in Fig. 9, and that these are more or less parallel to those drawn in the

[6] The markets M_1 and M_2 may be compared with "minorant" and "majorant" games Γ_1 and Γ_2 described in the J. von Neumann and O. Morgenstern, *Theory of Games and Economic Behavior* (Princeton: Princeton University Press, 1947), p. 100.

figure. If it is seller 1 who wants to force out seller 2, then 1 would try to bring down seller 2 to the region D and for that he would move his price towards the southwest.[7] But seller 2 can then counteract by moving in a northwesterly direction, thereby increasing his profits but decreasing 1's profits. Thus seller 1 cannot force 2 out of the market. The same thing is true if 2 wants to oust 1. Seller 2 will then move in a northwesterly direction but seller 1 can counteract by moving towards the northeast, thereby increasing his profits and also, incidentally, seller 2's profits. Hence we can conclude that in the situation depicted in Fig. 9, although seller 2 has an advantage, it is difficult for either seller to oust the other.

13.3.7. We have not said yet which constant price lines in Fig. 9 are higher and which are lower. We will see now that this ranking depends entirely on whether we assume that the goods are substitute goods or complementary goods. If we assume that the two sellers are selling rival goods (or, what is the same thing, substitutes), an increase in the price of one seller would increase the profits of the other seller, and vice versa. In Fig. 9, if seller 2 moves his price from 2.o to 2.a, seller 1's profits are increased and hence 2.a > 2.o > 2.b. Similarly, if seller 1 shifts his price from 1.o to 1.b, seller 2's profits are increased and therefore 1.b > 1.o > 1.a. If the two goods are complementary, the reverse of this process would be true and we would have 2.a < 2.o < 2.b and 1.b < 1.o < 1.a. When rival products are sold, 1 is said to be in α region and 2 in β region, where α and β regions are as classified in (13:E).

13.3.8. Let us look at the problem, making use of partial derivatives. In Fig. 9 the slopes of the p_1 curves are negative and those of the p_2 curves are positive, that is,

(13:2:a) $$\left(\frac{dg_2}{dg_1}\right)_{p_1} = \frac{\partial g_2/\partial p_2}{\partial g_1/\partial p_2} < 0,$$

(13:2:b) $$\left(\frac{dg_2}{dg_1}\right)_{p_2} = \frac{\partial g_2/\partial p_1}{\partial g_1/\partial p_1} > 0.[8]$$

[7] Meaning that he prefers the price lines which lie farther to the southwest.
[8] See Appendix C (C:6:a and b).

Assume now that the goods the two sellers sell are substitutes, then $\partial g_1/\partial p_2 > 0$ and $\partial g_2/\partial p_1 > 0$. Hence for (13:2:a) to be true, $\partial g_2/\partial p_2 < 0$; and for (13:2:b) to be true, $\partial g_1/\partial p_1 > 0$.

The first approximation of Taylor's expansion of the functions (13:1) about the initial prices $p_1{}^0$ and $p_2{}^0$ may be written in the following matrix form:[9]

$$
\begin{bmatrix} dg_1 \\ \\ dg_2 \end{bmatrix} = \begin{bmatrix} \dfrac{\partial g_1}{\partial p_1} & \dfrac{\partial g_1}{\partial p_2} \\ \\ \dfrac{\partial g_2}{\partial p_1} & \dfrac{\partial g_2}{\partial p_2} \end{bmatrix} \begin{bmatrix} dp_1 \\ \\ dp_2 \end{bmatrix}.
$$

The motives of the two sellers are to keep dg_1 greater than 0 and dg_2 greater than 0; as it is assumed that in this first case $\partial g_1/\partial p_1 > 0$, $\partial g_2/\partial p_2 < 0$, $\partial g_1/\partial p_2 > 0$ and $\partial g_2/\partial p_1 > 0$, seller 1 would keep dp_1 greater than 0 and seller 2 would keep dp_2 less than 0. In other words, seller 1 would increase his price and seller 2 would decrease his.

Thus we have the matrix solution as follows:

$$
\begin{bmatrix} dg_1 \\ \\ dg_2 \end{bmatrix} = \begin{bmatrix} \dfrac{\partial g_1}{\partial p_1} & \dfrac{\partial g_1}{\partial p_2} \\ \\ \dfrac{\partial g_2}{\partial p_1} & -\dfrac{\partial g_2}{\partial p_2} \end{bmatrix} \begin{bmatrix} dp_1 \\ \\ -dp_2 \end{bmatrix}.
$$

The square matrix in the center describes the structure of the market. The column matrix on the right-hand side shows the moves made by the sellers, that is, it shows that the signs before dp_1 and dp_2 are chosen by sellers 1 and 2, respectively.

We may note from the above matrix that seller 1 is in a disadvantageous position, because the negative dp_2 makes all the elements for dg_2 positive whereas it makes one element for dg_1

[9] For function $g_1 = g_1(p_1, p_2)$, the first approximation of Taylor's expansion about $p_1{}^0$ and $p_2{}^0$ is:

$$g_1(p_1, p_2) = g_1(p_1{}^0, p_2{}^0) + (p_1 - p_1{}^0)(\partial g_1/\partial p_1) + (p_2 - p_2{}^0)(\partial g_1/\partial p_2)$$

or $\quad g_1(p_1, p_2) - g_1(p_1{}^0, p_2{}^0) = (p_1 - p_1{}^0)(\partial g_1/\partial p_1) + (p_2 - p_2{}^0)(\partial g_1/\partial p_2)$

or $\quad\quad dg_1 = dp_1(\partial g_1/\partial p_1) + dp_2(\partial g_1/\partial p_2).$

negative. Hence dg_2 will always be positive, but dg_1 will be positive only when $\partial g_1/\partial p_1(dp_1) > \partial g_1/\partial p_2(dp_2)$.

This is why in Sec. 13.3.2 we use the expression "the best thing for seller 1 to do," meaning that seller 1's action will give him better profits than any other action would, but this does not necessarily mean that the action will make his profits larger than those obtained in the last situation. This feature should also be noticed in the other cases.

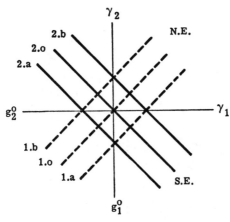

FIGURE 10

13.4. *The second case*

13.4.1. As our second case, we take Fig. 10. The original coordinates are not shown, but instead the transformed coordinates are drawn in the figure. It is substantially the same as Fig. 9 except that the naming of the curves is reversed, that is, the p_1 curves of Fig. 9 are now named p_2, and the p_2 curves of Fig. 9 have become p_1.

To increase the profits, seller 2 would move to the northeast and seller 1 to the southeast. It can be verified that statement (13:F) is valid in this case also. Moreover it can also be seen that the result would not be changed by applying either Cournot's or Stackelberg's conjectural variation. As in case 1, neither seller has power to oust the other seller. In contrast with case 1, however, it is now seller 2 who is at a disadvantage.

13.4.2. If the two sellers are selling rival commodities, then, as formulated in Sec. 13.3.7, we can say that 2.b > 2.o > 2.a and 1.b > 1.o > 1.a. Thus seller 2 is increasing his price when he moves towards the northeast to increase his profits, and seller 1 is cutting his price when he moves towards the

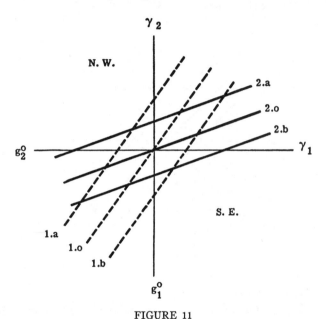

FIGURE 11

southeast. Seller 1 is in β region and seller 2 in α region. The matrix solution would in this case become[10]

$$
\begin{bmatrix} dg_1 \\ \\ dg_2 \end{bmatrix} = \begin{bmatrix} -\dfrac{\partial g_1}{\partial p_1} & \dfrac{\partial g_1}{\partial p_2} \\ \\ \dfrac{\partial g_2}{\partial p_1} & \dfrac{\partial g_2}{\partial p_2} \end{bmatrix} \begin{bmatrix} -dp_1 \\ \\ dp_2 \end{bmatrix}.
$$

[10] Unless noted specifically, we are considering the case of two sellers selling rival commodities.

13.5. *The third case*

The third case is represented in Fig. 11. To increase his profits, seller 1 would move towards the southeast and 2 would move towards the northwest. If they are selling rival goods, it means that they are increasing their prices to increase profits and the movement made by one seller benefits the other seller at the same time. Both are in α region. Statement (13:F) is valid and we can build in either Cournot's or Stackelberg's conjectural variation without changing the result obtained above.

Our matrix solution would be as follows:

$$
\begin{bmatrix} dg_1 \\ \\ dg_2 \end{bmatrix} = \begin{bmatrix} \dfrac{\partial g_1}{\partial p_1} & \dfrac{\partial g_1}{\partial p_2} \\ \\ \dfrac{\partial g_2}{\partial p_1} & \dfrac{\partial g_2}{\partial p_2} \end{bmatrix} \begin{bmatrix} dp_1 \\ \\ dp_2 \end{bmatrix}.
$$

13.6. *The fourth case*

The fourth case is represented in Fig. 12. Both are still in α region. To increase his profits, 1 would move towards the northwest and 2 would move towards the southeast, and if they are selling rival products, it means that both of them are increasing their prices.

The other results of Sec. 13.5, as well as the matrix solution of that section, hold true here.

13.7. *The fifth case*

13.7.1. Figure 13 represents the fifth case. It should be observed that the slopes of all the curves in cases 3 and 4 are positive, whereas in case 5 the slopes of these curves are negative.

At whatever value seller 2 fixes his price, it is most profitable for 1 to select 1.b. Similarly, whatever price 1 may fix, 2's profits are maximum if he fixes his price at 2.b. But we should note here that if seller 2 moves his price curve towards the northeast, seller 1's profits would be less than his initial profits. Seller 1 can then raise his profits by moving in a northeasterly direction, which may in turn decrease the profits of seller 2. Then 2 will move towards the northeast again.

If the two sellers are selling rival products, then by applying the rule of 13.3.7 we have $1.a > 1.o > 1.b$ and $2.a > 2.o > 2.b$. Thus moving in a northeasterly direction means that both sellers are cutting their prices.

It can be verified that statement (13:F) is valid and that if either of the conjectural variations of Cournot and Stackelberg is applied, we would still have the above solution.

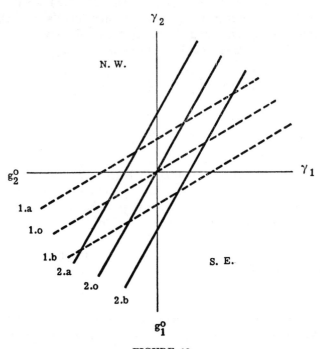

FIGURE 12

13.7.2. We may summarize the above result as follows: With the shapes and positions of the constant price curves as given in Fig. 13,[11] the most beneficial action that the two sellers can take is to cut their prices (if they are selling rival goods) or to increase their prices (if they are selling complementary goods). By doing so, they may both land in region A, B, or C, but never in region D.

[11] See Appendix D.

13.7.3. As defined in Sec. 13.2.2, each seller is in the β region. We will find later on that in the sixth case, each seller is still in region β, but the solution in that particular case is different from the solution in the present one. Let us therefore differentiate the two cases by saying that the two sellers in the present case are in the $\beta_1'\beta_2'$ region and that the two sellers in the next case are in the $\beta_1\beta_2$ region.

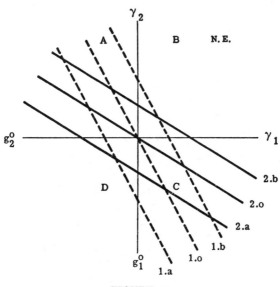

FIGURE 13

13.7.4. The matrix solution in this case is

$$\begin{bmatrix} dg_1 \\ \\ dg_2 \end{bmatrix} = \begin{bmatrix} -\dfrac{\partial g_1}{\partial p_1} & \dfrac{\partial g_1}{\partial p_2} \\ \\ \dfrac{\partial g_2}{\partial p_1} & -\dfrac{\partial g_2}{\partial p_2} \end{bmatrix} \begin{bmatrix} -dp_1 \\ \\ -dp_2 \end{bmatrix}.$$

13.8. *The sixth case*

13.8.1. The sixth case is represented in Fig. 14. All the curves are negatively inclined, as in Fig. 13, but in Fig. 14, the slopes of the p_1 curves are greater than those of the p_2 curves.

If seller 2 fixes his price at 2.a or 2.o or 2.b, the most profitable price for seller 1 is 1.a. If seller 1 fixes his price at 1.a, 1.o, or 1.b, the most profitable price for seller 2 is 2.a. But if seller 2 selects this value of 2.a, and seller 1 selects 1.a, we see from the above figure that they would land in region D. This would then mean a decrease in profit for both sellers.

Let us now see whether this result would be changed if we

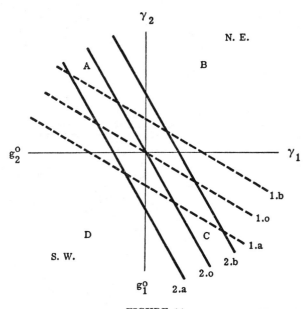

FIGURE 14

apply either Cournot's conjectural variation or Stackelberg's. According to Cournot, seller 1 would select 1.a for he would assume that 2 will remain at 2.o; seller 2 would select price 2.a assuming 1 will remain at price 1.o. Hence the above result is not changed.

We will get the same result if we apply Stackelberg's conjectural variation. In market M_1, seller 1 assumes that 2 will maximize profits for any price that 1 has selected, that is, if 1 selects 1.a, 2 will select 2.a; if 1 selects 1.b, 2 will again select 2.a. Under these circumstances, the best that 1 can do is to select 1.a. In market M_2, seller 2 assumes that 1 will maximize profits for any price selected by 2, that is, that 1 will select 1.a for any price selected by 2. Seller 2 will then select 2.a, which is the best for him under these circumstances. So we see that both markets, M_1 and M_2, give the same result as above.

In both Cournot's and Stackelberg's cases, if the nature of the conjectural variations is not changed, seller 1 will *keep moving* towards the southwest, thinking that such action will increase his profits.[12] Similarly, seller 2 will also *keep moving* towards the southwest. Thus they will go deeper and deeper into region D, their profits decreasing more and more.

We cannot say that this behavior of the sellers is rational, as the result of their behavior is contrary to the motive that we assumed in Sec. 13.1.2(A). Hence we must change the conjectural variations.

13.8.2. In Fig. 14, at prices 1.b and 2.b, both sellers are in region B. We must find out what assumptions or conjectures will lead the sellers to select these two prices. In market M_1, if 1 has to select first and he chooses 1.b, the profits of 2 increase whereas the profits of 1 decrease. Seller 2 will not of his own accord bring his price up to 2.b; rather, he will decrease his price to 2.a. Hence 1 will not move to 1.b on his own. The same thing happens in market M_2 where 2 selects his price first. If he selects 2.b, his own profits decrease while 1's profits increase and 1 will be in no mood to increase his price to 1.b of his own accord. Hence 2 loses and therefore will not move to 2.b of his own accord.

In each of the five cases (Secs. 13.3 to 13.7), we found that (13:F) was true and that the two sellers could act independently and still increase their profits, but in the sixth case it would not be possible for them to accomplish this. Instead, they have to come to some kind of agreement.[13] That is, 1 will increase his

---

[12] If the two sellers are selling rival products, 2.b > 2.o > 2.a and 1.b > 1.o > 1.a. In the above results, the statement that the sellers are moving towards the southwest means that both are cutting their prices.

[13] An understanding or tacit agreement in this case need not involve actual price fixing but may only mean that if one increases his price the other will follow suit.

price to 1.b only if there is an understanding that 2 will follow suit, and if 2 is to act first he will increase his price to 2.b on the understanding that 1 will also increase his price later.[14]

13.8.3. As mentioned in 13.7.3, we will say for the present case that the two sellers are in $\beta_1\beta_2$ region. It is to be noted here that differentiation between β and β' is necessary only when there is more than one seller in the β region.

13.8.4. Our matrix solution for this problem is then

$$\begin{bmatrix} dg_1 \\ dg_2 \end{bmatrix} = \begin{bmatrix} -\dfrac{\partial g_1}{\partial p_1} & \dfrac{\partial g_1}{\partial p_2} \\ \dfrac{\partial g_2}{\partial p_1} & -\dfrac{\partial g_2}{\partial p_2} \end{bmatrix} \begin{bmatrix} dp_1 \\ dp_2 \end{bmatrix}.$$

14. THE FULL MARKET WITH TWO SELLERS

14.1. *The assumptions and the characteristics*

14.1.1. The six cases discussed in Sec. 13 are simplified "partial" markets. In those cases, as explained in Sec. 13.2.2, we find only one region, either α or β, for each seller throughout the whole market. In the present section we will admit both these regions α and β for our sellers and we will call such a market a "full market" to differentiate it from the "partial markets" of Sec. 13.

We will assume that the two sellers in the market sell differentiated products as in Sec. 13 and that the products are substitutes for each other. As we are admitting all the possible regions into this "full market," the constant price curves will take the shape shown in Fig. 15.

The constant p_1 curves are represented by broken lines and are denoted by 1.a, 1.b, 1.c, etc., where 1.a $<$ 1.b $<$ 1.c $< \ldots$, and the constant p curves are represented by continuous lines and are denoted by 2.a, 2.b, 2.c, etc., where 2.a $<$ 2.b $<$ 2.c $< \ldots$. In the family of constant p_1 curves, the price levels of the curves rise as we move upward from the abscissa; and in the family of the constant p_2 curves, the price levels of the curves rise as we

---

[14] See Appendix E for the mathematical treatment of this case.

move to the right from the ordinate. The maxima of the p_1 curves as measured from the abscissa are joined by the curve uu', and the maxima of the p_2 curves as measured from the ordinate are joined by the curve vv'.

If we move up along any constant p_2 curve, we will find that as the p_2 curve is concave towards the vertical axis, the g_1 values of the curve increase first until the vv' curve is reached and that after this, g_1 decreases. At the same time, moving up along a p_2 curve, we pass through higher and higher values of p_1. These two facts taken together mean that with p_2 constant, the profits of the first seller increase, reach a maximum, and then decrease as his price increases. According to the classification of Sec. 13.2.2, seller 1 is in region α_1 when he is below the vv' curve, and in region β_1 when he is above the vv' curve.

Similarly, for seller 2, if we move along any constant p_1 curve, we will find that as the p_1 curve is concave towards the horizontal axis, the g_2 values of the curve increase first until the uu' curve is reached and that after this, g_2 decreases. At the same time, moving up along a p_1 curve, we pass through higher and higher values of p_2. The two facts combined mean that with p_1 constant, g_2 increases, reaches a maximum, and then decreases as seller 2's price increases. Hence seller 2 is in region α_2 when he is on the left-hand side of the uu' curve and he is in region β_2 when he is on the right-hand side.

We are also assuming that the curves are smooth as drawn in the figure, that uu' is concave towards the ordinate with an extreme point at L_1, and that vv' is concave towards the abscissa with an extreme point at L_2.

We are further assuming that the joint profits of the two sellers are not unlimited, in other words, with g_1 constant at any level, there is a maximum value for g_2 that 2 can obtain, and similarly for any given value of g_2, there is a maximum value for g_1.[15] Thus in Fig. 15, we have an envelope curve uv', the significance of which will be fully explained later.

Looking at Fig. 15, we find that some of the constant p_1 and p_2 curves come to an abrupt end when they reach the envelope curve uv'. Actually they do not end there; but to draw the re-

[15] See Appendix F.

maining portions of the curves in Fig. 15 would be confusing to the eye, and so we have drawn these remaining portions of the curves in Fig. 16. If we superimpose Fig. 16 on Fig. 15, we find that the uv' curve of Fig. 16 falls on the uv' curve of Fig. 15 and that the half-finished curves of Fig. 16 will be flush with their remaining portions drawn in Fig. 15. Thus the whole of the con-

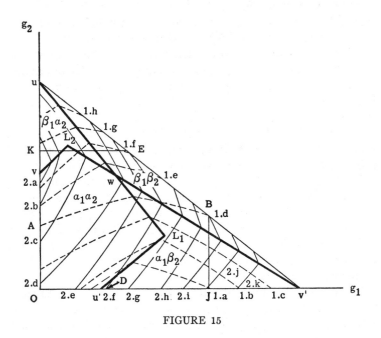

FIGURE 15

stant p_1 curve ABC is made up by a composite of part AB in Fig. 15 and part BC in Fig. 16.

The constant p_2 curves are treated in a similar way. For example the curve DEF is represented in part by DE in Fig. 15 and in part by EF in Fig. 16. As in Fig. 15, the p_1 curves are drawn in broken lines and the p_2 curves are drawn in continuous lines in Fig. 16. The values of both the constant p_1 and p_2 curves decrease as we move up from the origin.

In Fig. 15, at any value of g_1, say OJ, if we move up from J along the line JB, the profits of the second seller increase, but the increase comes to a stop at B, when the envelope curve uv' is reached. Moving up along the line JB means the same thing as keeping profits g_1 constant and increasing price p_1. After we have reached B, if we still want to keep the profits of seller 1 at OJ and go on increasing p_1, we will have to proceed to Fig. 16 and move downward along the line BJ of that figure, and as we move down we will pass through higher and higher levels of p_1 but lower and lower values of g_2.

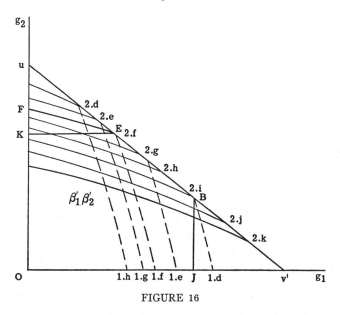

FIGURE 16

Similarly, in Fig. 15, if we keep g_2 constant at the level of OK and move along KE from K, we find that p_2 increases and at the same time g_1 also increases until we reach E. If from E we want to go on increasing p_2, we proceed to Fig. 16 and move left along the line EK from E and then we will find that we pass through higher and higher values of p_2 curves but lower and lower values of g_1.

Thus though Fig. 16 represents the β regions for sellers 1 and 2, the characteristics of the β regions in Fig. 16 are different from those of the β regions in Fig. 15. We will designate these two regions β_1' and β_2' for sellers 1 and 2, respectively, as in Sec. 13.7.3.

14.1.2. Figure 15 is divided into four regions by the curves uu' and vv'. In region uvw (w being the intersection point of curves uu' and vv'), we find that 1 is in the β_1 category and 2 in the α_2 category; hence we will call this region $\beta_1\alpha_2$. In a similar way, region uwv' will be called region $\beta_1\beta_2$, $u'wv'$ will be called region $\alpha_1\beta_2$, and region vwu' will be called $\alpha_1\alpha_2$. The whole of Fig. 16 will be called region $\beta_1'\beta_2'$.

When we compare the shapes and characteristics of the constant price curves in these various regions with those of the six cases described in Sec. 13, we find that

case 1 belongs to region $\alpha_1\beta_2$,
case 2 belongs to region $\beta_1\alpha_2$,
case 3 belongs to region $\alpha_1\alpha_2$,
case 4 belongs to region $\alpha_1\alpha_2$,
case 5 belongs to region $\beta_1'\beta_2'$,
case 6 belongs to region $\beta_1\beta_2$.

14.2. *The rational behavior*

14.2.1. We are assuming that each of the two sellers realizes the existence of such regions as α and β. Each will also know which of these regions he is in at a given moment through having in the past experienced and studied changes in his profits resulting from price changes. For the time being, we will also assume that each seller knows which region the other seller is in at any given time. This assumption is discussed in Sec. 14.2.8.

We saw in Sec. 13 the significance and the characteristics of the various regions of α and β. In the light of these results, let us now see how the two sellers would act in different situations.

14.2.2. First let us take the region $\alpha_1\alpha_2$. At any point in this region, both sellers would increase their prices, and this would also increase the profits of both. Their action may however deposit them in any one of the four other regions. The question now arising is, which region would each seller like to be in? Looking at Fig. 15, we see that the $\alpha_1\beta_2$ region would give more profits for 1 while the $\beta_1\alpha_2$ region would give 2 a similar increase in profits compared to the profits that these sellers would get in the $\alpha_1\alpha_2$ region. We will find, however, that neither of these regions provide stable situations for 1 and 2.

14.2.3. Let us now take region $\beta_1\alpha_2$. We found in Sec. 13.4 above that in this region, in order for seller 1 to increase his profits, he would have to decrease his price, which would affect 2 adversely, so that 2, to make up his loss, would have to increase his price, thus increasing 1's profits still further. Seller 1, with some clever manipulation, can bring both himself and seller 2 to position w or an approximation thereof. In order to extricate himself from such a disadvantageous position, seller 2 can do one of two things: he can either try to get out of region $\beta_1\alpha_2$ without adversely affecting seller 1 or he can follow a retaliatory policy.

Let us first consider the possibility of getting out of region $\beta_1\alpha_2$. The next best place for seller 2 to be in is region $\beta_1\beta_2$. Of course, seller 2 would have to increase his price; but if he increases the price by too small an amount, he may still remain in $\beta_1\alpha_2$ or else he may land in $\alpha_1\alpha_2$, depending upon the extent of the price cut made by 1. If 2 increases his price too much, he may "overprice" his product, that is, he may land in region $\beta_1'\beta_2'$, especially if 1 does not make a substantial cut in his own price. Such considerations would thus limit 2's freedom to increase his price.

The other alternative for 2, as mentioned above, is to retaliate for the price cut made by 1 by cutting his own price. When 2 cuts his price, not only will 1's profits decrease but 2's will also. However, seller 1 will not be able to raise his profits to the old level, and the most he can do is to try to get on the vv' curve, which would give him the maximum profits for the price fixed by 2. The victor in this kind of price war will be the one whose financial position is stronger and who has probably reaped a large harvest of profits in previous years, enabling him to bear the current loss.

14.2.4. The $\alpha_1\beta_2$ region is just the reverse case of region $\beta_1\alpha_2$. If the sellers are in region $\alpha_1\beta_2$, as we saw in Sec. 13.3, seller 2 would decrease his price; seller 1 would increase his price and place himself in a disadvantageous position. The same analysis of Sec. 14.2.3 would apply in this case if we interchange seller 1 for 2 and seller 2 for 1 in the previous section.

14.2.5. If the sellers are in region $\beta_1\beta_2$, then the analysis of Sec. 13.8 applies. It will be to the interest of both sellers to come to some kind of agreement or understanding so that both of them could increase their prices and thus increase their profits. But in increasing their prices, they would have to be cautious not to "overprice" their products, that is, not to land in region $\beta_1'\beta_2'$.

14.2.6. If the sellers are in region $\beta_1'\beta_2'$, the analysis in Sec. 13.7 applies. They would both cut their prices so as to go back to region $\beta_1\beta_2$. The effect of this price cutting would be an increase of profits for either seller before or after the other seller has cut his price. As price cutting is thus beneficial to both, they do not need to come to any agreement for such an action.

14.2.7. If we study Figs. 15 and 16 very carefully, we will find that region $\beta_1\beta_2$ is the ultimate for both sellers and that line uv' of Figs. 15 and 16 gives the optimum line for the sellers, that is, whenever the two sellers are in region $\beta_1\beta_2$, they would tend to move in the direction of line uv'. The particular point at which both sellers are to be found depends on the ability of the sellers to negotiate with each other.

We have seen in Secs. 14.2.2, 14.2.3, 14.2.4, and 14.2.6 that regions $\alpha_1\alpha_2$, $\beta_1\alpha_2$, $\alpha_1\beta_2$, and $\beta_1'\beta_2'$ are not stable regions for the sellers. Their actions would lead them ultimately to region $\beta_1\beta_2$.

Thus region $\beta_1\beta_2$ is what we shall call the stable region, where with perfect understanding the two sellers will be increasing their prices either at the same time or one after the other.

14.2.8. Thus far, we have assumed in Sec. 14.2.1 that each seller knows which region (whether α or β) the other seller is in at any given time. If either seller does not know this exactly, he would make a conjecture. If he should find that his first guess is wrong, then, through a process of trial and error, he would soon learn the correct region. There can, of course, be the extreme case where the regions occupied by the two sellers keep changing as both the sellers move and as each is mistaken in assuming what the other seller's region is.

We can also have the case of a mistaken assumption by one seller with the other seller playing along with the first seller's mistake to his own advantage. For such a case, we may assume that seller 1 is in the β region and 2 in the α region but that seller 1 is mistakenly assuming that 2 is also in the β region. If seller 1 approaches 2 for an agreement to increase the price, then it is to 2's advantage to play along with 1's mistake and to pretend that he is in the β region.

14.2.9. The above discussion has presented a static analysis where the functions g_1 and g_2 and, consequently, the graphs of Figs. 15 and 16 also are considered to remain unchanged. As the demand changes as a result of changes in products or advertising or as a result of other outside forces such as income, the functions and the figures will change. Let us consider a few cases here:

(a) Let us assume that other sellers have come into the market and that the market structure has therefore changed. The newcomers to the market are selling hitherto unknown and unpopular brands; hence they will try to price their products below those of sellers 1 and 2. If the buyers change over to the newcomers, thereby causing a change in the demand situation facing the two original sellers, then these two sellers may find themselves in region $\beta_1'\beta_2'$ rather than in $\beta_1\beta_2$. The move results from the fact that with the contraction of the demand for sellers 1 and 2, the curve uv' shifts downward, and if the two sellers happen to be very near the uv' curve (which they would be as they are old sellers and may, through successive agreements, have raised their prices too high), they would be left out of $\beta_1\beta_2$ and would be in $\beta_1'\beta_2'$. When they are in the latter region, they would both cut their prices and try to be in the $\beta_1\beta_2$ region again since that would be the only way of increasing their profits.

(b) Let us now take the case of a recession setting in. In this event, with decreased income and employment, the demand would come down, changing Fig. 15 in such a way that the curves would contract, that is, the uv' curve would move downward, seller 1's price lines would move down, and seller 2's price lines would move westward. This result is shown in Fig. 17. As in Fig. 15, g_2 and g_1 are represented by the ordinate and abscissa respectively. Here 1_0 and 2_0 belong to the family of constant price curves of the initial period and represent the constant price curves of sellers 1 and 2, respectively, while r_0 represents the position of the two sellers at the initial period 0; 1_1 and 2_1 represent the constant price curves of sellers 1 and 2, respectively, and r_1 represents the position of the two sellers at period 1. The envelope curve u_0v_0' at time 0 moves down to u_1v_1' at period 1.

We observe from Fig. 17 that at r_1 the profits of both sellers have decreased. If the sellers want to derive the same level of profits that they were getting in the initial period 0, they must shift their position back to r_0.[16] In the family of constant price curves of period 1, the price curves of sellers 1 and 2 passing through r_0 would be higher than those of period 1. Hence there

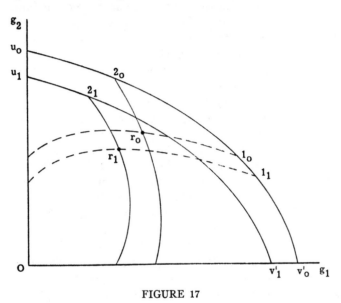

FIGURE 17

will be an increase in the prices of both sellers in period 1 although the demand has contracted. The extent to which the sellers would increase their prices depends on the new envelope curve u_1v_1'. If this is very close to r_1, not much of a price rise is possible as it would mean that they would be overpricing their products and would be in the $\beta_1'\beta_2'$ region.

(c) If the two sellers are situated in the $\beta_1\beta_2$ region and are very close to the envelope curve u_1v_1', then it would not be pos-

[16] If r_0 is outside of the new envelope curve u_1v_1', the sellers cannot get the profits that they used to get in the initial period.

sible for their profits to be increased unless the envelope curve shifts upward. Changes in the nature of the product and the "advertising outlays"[17] are devices in the hands of the sellers to shift the u_1v_1' curve upward.

[17] The two terms are here used in the sense described by Chamberlin. See Chamberlin, *Monopolistic Competition*, Chapter V, Section 1.

CHAPTER V

The Theory Extended to More Than Two Sellers

15. THE CASE OF FOUR SELLERS

15.1.1. In Sec. 13.2.2, it was pointed out that a seller can at any moment be in region α, where $\partial g_0/\partial p_0 > 0$, or in region β, where $\partial g_0/\partial p_0 < 0$. Coming to the case of two sellers, we saw in Sec. 14 that the two sellers can be in any one of the following possible regions:

$$\alpha_1\beta_2, \quad \alpha_1\alpha_2, \quad \beta_1\beta_2, \quad \beta_1\alpha_2, \quad \beta_1'\beta_2'.$$

The behaviors of the sellers were then analyzed according to the regions they were in at the moment.

15.1.2. We may follow the same procedure in cases where there are more than two sellers. Let us now take the case of four sellers as an example. It is first necessary to give all the possible combinations of α,β regions that the sellers can be occupying at any moment. Excluding the β' regions, the following are all the possible combinations of α,β regions open to the four sellers:[1]

Sellers 1	2	3	4	1	2	3	4	1	2	3	4	1	2	3	4
α	β	β	β	α	α	β	β	β	α	β	β	β	β	β	β
α	β	α	α	α	α	α	α	β	α	α	α	β	β	α	α
α	β	α	β	α	α	α	β	β	α	α	β	β	β	α	β
α	β	β	α	α	α	β	α	β	α	β	α	β	β	β	α

Group A: The cases of $\alpha\alpha\alpha\alpha$ and $\beta\beta\beta\beta$ are comparable to $\alpha\alpha$ and $\beta\beta$ of two sellers, respectively. In the case of $\alpha\alpha\alpha\alpha$, it would

[1] The subscripts to α and β are dropped for the sake of convenience. In a combination, the first letter stands for seller 1, the second stands for seller 2, the third stands for seller 3 and the fourth stands for seller 4. Thus $\alpha_1\beta_2\beta_3\alpha_4$ is abbreviated to $\alpha\beta\beta\alpha$.

be to every seller's interest to increase his price, and through this move, everyone's profits would increase and the sellers do not need to come to an agreement. In the case of $\beta\beta\beta\beta$, if each seller acts independently and cuts his price, everyone's profits would decrease and hence each would have to increase his price to get an increase in profits, but a seller by himself will not do so unless he understands that the others will follow his example. In this case, a tacit agreement is required.[2]

Group B: Cases $\alpha\beta\alpha\alpha$, $\alpha\alpha\alpha\beta$, $\beta\alpha\alpha\alpha$, $\alpha\alpha\beta\alpha$, in each of which there is only one β, are similar to cases $\alpha\beta$ and $\beta\alpha$ of two sellers. The seller in the β region would decrease his price and that would adversely affect the sellers in α region. The latter would increase their prices.

Group C: Cases $\alpha\beta\beta\beta$, $\alpha\beta\alpha\beta$, $\alpha\beta\beta\alpha$, $\alpha\alpha\beta\beta$, $\beta\alpha\beta\beta$, $\beta\alpha\alpha\beta$, $\beta\alpha\beta\alpha$, $\beta\beta\alpha\alpha$, $\beta\beta\alpha\beta$, $\beta\beta\beta\alpha$ are not directly comparable to any of those in the market with two sellers. In this group, there are two or more sellers in region β and if they are to act independently, each will cut his price, which would lead to a decrease in the profits of all the sellers in β region. Hence, as in the case of $\beta\beta$ with two sellers, the sellers in the β region will come to a tacit agreement and they will all increase their prices. Those sellers in the α region will of course increase their prices, and this will have a favorable effect on all the sellers in the group. Thus, in this group, all the sellers come to increase their prices — those in the β region after reaching a tacit agreement and those in the α region without the need for such an agreement.

15.1.3. We have seen in the case of two sellers that if *both* sellers are in the β' region, each seller is in the β region[3] but an increase in price on the part of each seller would not increase the profits of both as in the $\beta\beta$ region. If the β' regions are introduced, the following groups may be listed:[4]

Group D: Cases in this group are to be formed by substituting β' for β in the cases of group C. The sellers in the β' region would

---

[2] An understanding or tacit agreement in this case need not involve actual price fixing but may only mean that if one increases his price the other will follow suit.

[3] β' is a subset of β.

[4] Those cases including β' that are mentioned in this section are by no means exhaustive.

cut their prices without the need to reach an agreement, and this act would be unfavorable to those in region α, who would have to increase their prices to increase their profits.

Group E: The case in this group can be formed by substituting β' for β in the case of $\beta\beta\beta\beta$ of group A. In this case, every seller would decrease his price without the need for a tacit agreement.

Group F: This group consists of cases having two sellers in the β region and the remaining two in the β' region. The sellers in the β' region would decrease their prices and those in the β region would, after coming to a tacit agreement, increase their prices.

It is to be noted that in some cases in groups D and E, there may be a very small seller in the β region, a price movement on whose part may not significantly affect the other sellers. In such a case, the seller may conjecture that even if he were to decrease his price, the other sellers would not follow suit. In this type of case, we may find this seller decreasing his price.

CHAPTER VI

Conclusions

16. COURNOT'S AND STACKELBERG'S CASES RECONSIDERED

16.1. *Cournot's case reconsidered*

If we examine Fig. 18, which is of the same type as Fig. 15, we will see that for any given price line of 2, seller 1 will obtain maximum profits if he selects the price line that passes through the intersection of 2's present price line and the vv' curve. Thus vv' corresponds to Cournot's reaction curve for seller 1. Similarly, for any given price line of 1, seller 2's profits are maximum if he selects the price line passing through the intersection of 1's present price line and the uu' curve. Thus uu' corresponds to Cournot's reaction curve for seller 2.

Cournot's equilibrium is reached at w, where uu' and vv' intersect. To explain how this equilibrium is reached and also to consider the implications of this solution, let us assume that the initial position of the two sellers is at the point E in Fig. 18. At the point E, the prices of sellers 1 and 2 are given by the value of price lines 1.a and 2.a, respectively, and the profits of 1 and 2 are given by the horizontal magnitude of E and the vertical magnitude of E, respectively.

According to Cournot, at the point E, if 1 is to act first,[1] he would select the price line 1.b that goes through A_1 because 1 assumes that 2 will keep his present price 2.a constant and, on that assumption, the point A_1 on 2.a and vv' would give seller 1 the best profits. Seller 2 would then select the price line 2.b going through A_2 because 2 assumes that 1 will keep his present price

---

[1] As opposed to "continuous analysis," the presentation here is a "step-by-step analysis," in which the variables, that is, the prices and profits, move discontinuously in distinct time intervals. It is also assumed that points A_1, A_2, . . . are reached without a necessity for "hunting."

1.b constant and, on that assumption, the point A_2 on 1.b and uu' gives seller 2 the best profits. Then, by a similar process, 1 selects the price line 1.c that goes through A_3. This alternation of action goes on until the equilibrium point w is reached. In Fig. 18, the prices 1.a > 1.b > 1.c > 1.d and 2.a > 2.b > 2.c.

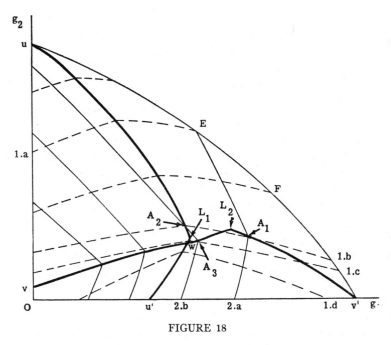

FIGURE 18

Hence the above solution means that from the point E both the sellers cut their prices.

16.2. Stackelberg's case reconsidered

Let us first consider the case where seller 1 is the follower and 2 the leader. As the follower, seller 1 will take 2's ruling price as fixed and will maximize his profits accordingly. In other words, in Fig. 18, given 2's price line, seller 1 will choose the price line that passes through the point where vv' and 2's price line intersect. If 2 knows that 1 will always choose this line, that is, if 2 knows or conjectures that both sellers will always end up on the vv' curve, he will choose the point L_2 since that would give him the best profits possible under the circumstances.

Let us now consider the case where seller 2 is the follower and 1 the leader. As the follower, seller 2 will take 1's ruling price as fixed and will maximize his profits accordingly. In other words, in Fig. 18, given 1's price line, seller 2 will choose the price line passing through the point where uu' and 1's price line intersect. If 1 knows or conjectures that 2 will always take this course of action, that is, if 1 knows that both sellers will always end up on the uu' curve, he will choose the point L_1 since that gives him the best profits under the circumstances.

Stackelberg assumes that each seller compares his profits under the conditions of the two positions L_1 and L_2 and that he chooses the one that gives him the greater profits. According to Fig. 18, both sellers will choose L_2 since their profits in that position are greater than those in L_1. Thus L_2 is the equilibrium position for Stackelberg.

If we look at Fig. 15, seller 1 is better off in position L_1 and seller 2 is better off in position L_2. Here both act as leaders and, according to Stackelberg, no equilibrium position can be attained.

16.3. *Conclusions*

In the case of Cournot, we saw that although the initial point may be at either E or F in Fig. 18, both sellers will continue to cut their prices in spite of the fact that in doing so the profits of both will be decreased. The sellers will come to a stop only at w.

In the case of Stackelberg, we found also that even if the initial position of the two sellers is at F in Fig. 18, they will not stay at this position but will come down to the point L_2, where the profits of both are less than those obtained while at F.

With these fixed conjectures, therefore, we see each of the sellers taking up a certain line of action which brings about a result quite contrary to the result aimed at, namely, the obtaining of better profits for everyone. Another line of action is possible for each seller that would lead him to the result he desires. As pointed out in Sec. 13.8.1, the above behavior on the part of both sellers, in leading them to results opposite to those originally aimed at, can be termed irrational behavior.

In Sec. 18, these cases of fixed conjectures are compared to feedback system control.

17. CHAMBERLIN'S AND FELLNER'S CASES RECONSIDERED

17.1. *Chamberlin's case reconsidered*

Let us now consider the graphic solutions of Chamberlin and Fellner, using Fig. 19, which is of the same type as Fig. 15. Figure 19 complies with Professor Chamberlin's assumptions of the uniformity of the demand curves as described in Sec. 9.1.2.

In Fig. 19, OA represents the 45-degree line between the two coordinates, and at all points on that line, equal profits will be enjoyed by both the sellers. The assumptions of uniformity of

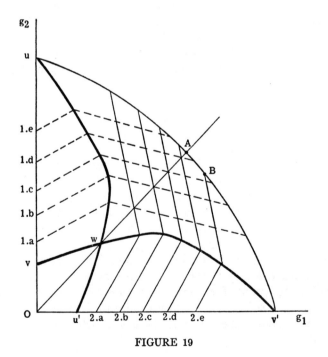

FIGURE 19

Professor Chamberlin call for the following features in Fig. 19.
(17:A) The price lines that intersect on the 45-degree line OA
are of equal magnitude;[1] prices 1.a = 2.a, 1.b = 2.b, 1.c = 2.c,
1.d = 2.d, etc. This means that if the two sellers charge the same
price, the same quantity will be sold and the same amount of
profit will be obtained by both sellers.

(17:B) If seller 1 fixes a certain price, say 1.a, then the profits
that he will get when seller 2 sells at 2.a, 2.b, 2.c, . . . would be
the same as the profits that seller 2 gets when he fixes his price
at 2.a, and seller 1 sells at 1.a, 1.b, 1.c, . . . , respectively. In
other words, $g_1(1.a, 2.d) = g_2(1.d, 2.a)$.

Professor Chamberlin does not state his solution explicitly.
He says only, "If each sought to maximize his profit with regard
for his full influence, direct and indirect, upon the situation, the
price BQ, yielding the maximum total profits to all, would be
set."[2] The line OA in Fig. 19 corresponds to the demand curve
DD' of Fig. 4. The point A in Fig. 19 corresponds to Professor
Chamberlin's equilibrium point because A is on the envelope
curve uv', and if the two sellers are to charge equal prices, they
cannot attain more profits than those represented by A.

The question now is, why should the sellers choose the demand
curve DD' or, what is the same thing, line OA? Professor Chamberlin's two assumptions — the assumption of uniformity in the
demand curves, and the assumption of recognition by the two
sellers of "mutual dependence" — are not sufficient conditions
to make the two sellers choose the line OA and attain the equilibrium point at A. They may choose some other line and attain
equilibrium at any other point, say at B, where B is on the
envelope curve.

17.2. Fellner's case reconsidered

Professor Fellner's solution gives an equilibrium point on the
envelope curve uv', and the particular point on the uv' curve is

---

[1] Prices 1.a, 1.b, . . . represent seller 1's prices and prices 2.a, 2.b, . . . represent
seller 2's prices. Curves 1.a, and 2.a, 3.a, . . . are symmetrical about the 45-degree
line OA.

[2] E. H. Chamberlin, *The Theory of Monopolistic Competition*, 7th edition (Cambridge, Mass.: Harvard University Press, 1956), p. 100. The price BQ is shown in
Fig. 4 above.

determined by the proportion of the shares in which the sellers have agreed to divide the profits among themselves. In Fig. 19, if the sellers agree to share profits equally, the point at which line OA and the uv' curve intersect is the equilibrium point. The position of line OA is given by the proportion of the shares in which the sellers have agreed to divide the profits among themselves, and if this proportion of shared profits changes, the position of line OA changes, and the intersection of this line and uv' will continue to give the equilibrium position.

17.3. *Conclusions*

17.3. Both Professor Chamberlin and Professor Fellner come to the conclusion that the result in oligopoly is that the two sellers share profits. Chamberlin emphasizes that to get this result the sellers need not go into "tacit agreement" and that even if they act independently the same result will be obtained. Fellner's position is different. His result is directly obtained by the assumption that the sellers come to an agreement to share their profits in some definite proportion.

In our discussion, it was shown that only in some cases, namely, when at least two sellers are in the β region, some kind of agreement, which needs to be merely an understanding that each seller will increase his price, is necessary. In other cases, such as $\alpha\alpha$ or $\alpha\beta$, no agreement is necessary.

18. APPLICATION OF THE FEEDBACK PRINCIPLE TO OLIGOPOLY PROBLEMS

18.1. *The principle of feedback*

18.1.1. In this section the principles of feedback or servo-mechanism are used to explain the various oligopoly theories described earlier. Before proceeding to the application of this theory, we shall review its principles briefly.

18.1.2. Many good designs for electrical apparatus incorporate the principle of feedback,[3] which engineers have been

---

[3] Gordon S. Brown and Donald P. Campbell, *Principles of Servo-mechanisms* (New York: Wiley, 1950) Chapters 1 and 2; see also the articles in *Scientific American*, Sept. 1952, on the principle of feedback.

using for quite some time. Only in the last decade or so, however, has the principle been recognized and the theory of designs formulated.

The principle of feedback is applied mainly to control mechanisms, with the result that to many people feedback and automatic control are synonymous. Automatic control need not incorporate feedback, however. In order to have feedback, we must have a closed-loop system. (In an open-loop system, there is nothing in the mechanism which connects the input with the output or which measures the result of the control operation and changes the result if it is not what is desired.) The essential requirement of closed-loop control is that the error between the state desired (input) and the state produced (output) is constantly measured, and if there is an error (difference between input and output) something is done about it. A closed-loop control system is thus an error-sensitive system. In other words, the open-loop system operates without a knowledge of the precision it attains during operation while, in contrast, the closed-loop system operates in terms of an error and tends at all times to minimize the error in the closed loop.

Time-operated traffic lights are one example of open-loop control since the volume of the traffic cannot affect the time mechanism that actuates the lights. An automatic clothes washer is another example of open-loop control, for the degree of dirtiness of the clothes cannot affect the duration of the time they remain in the washer.

18.1.3. The control system that is used in this section may be described as a step-by-step one.[4] As opposed to continuous control, in *step-by-step control* the potential correction is applied discontinuously at distinct time intervals. If the amount of change of potential correction is independent of the deviation causing the correcting action, the control may be called *deviation independent step-by-step control*. The subsequent investigations

[4] Hans Sartorius, "Deviation Dependent Step-by-Step Control Systems and Their Stability," *Conference on Automatic Control, Cranfield, Eng., 1951* (London: Butterworth's Scientific Publications, 1952), pp. 421–434. R. C. Oldenbourg, "Deviation Dependent Step-by-Step Control as Means to Achieve Optimum Control for Plants with Large Distance-velocity Lag," *Conference on Automatic Control*, pp. 435–447.

are restricted to step-by-step control in which the change of potential correction is dependent on the deviation, and the control may be called *deviation dependent step-by-step control*.

The equidistant time intervals are represented by $T - 1$, T, $T + 1, \ldots$.

18.2. *Oligopoly theories with fixed conjectures and with price as a controlled quantity*

We will now apply the feedback principle to the oligopoly theories with fixed conjectures, such as the theories of Cournot, Stackelberg, and Smithies, and those theories that use the type of conjectural dependence described in Sec. 5.5.

In the theories listed above, the control system (that is, the prescription for the behavior of the sellers) is designed as follows:

In Fig. 20, the control system is shown for seller 1. There is a conjecture box for him and the properties of that box remain fixed throughout. At the initial state, the values of the prices of other sellers are fed into the conjecture box, and the box tells its owner-designer what prices he should expect the other sellers to

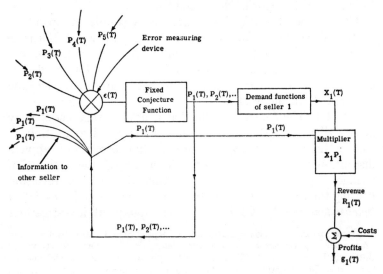

FIGURE 20

decide on and, under these circumstances, what price he himself should fix in order to get maximum profits. In the next period, the prices expected of the other sellers are compared with the prices that are actually fixed by them. If the error-measuring device finds an error, it is fed into the conjecture box which gives anew the prices to be expected of the other sellers and also the price which the seller in question should fix. This process is repeated until the stationary state is reached when the error becomes zero, that is, when the prices expected of the other sellers as given by the box are the same as the actual prices fixed by them.

The profit calculation is shown on the right-hand side of the diagram as an open end which is not fed back. This design is obviously a bad one because the error that is controlled is the error in price rather than in profit. This is the reason that, in the various theories listed above, the profits of the sellers in the stationary state (equilibrium position) may be far less than those at the initial position.

18.3. Oligopoly theory using multiple conjecture functions and with profits as a controlled quantity

18.3.1. The design in 18.2 can be improved if,

(18:A) $\Delta g(T)$ or dg/dt is fed back into the system,

(18:B) the properties of the conjecture box, instead of remaining fixed, are allowed to change, and the selection of a particular conjecture function is influenced by $\Delta g(T)$ or dg/dt.

It will be found that with the incorporation of these two improvements, the control system has the properties of the solution that were put forward in Secs. 14 and 15.

18.3.2. The improved design for seller 1 is shown in Fig. 21. In the lower part of the figure, the boxes $f_{1a}, f_{1b}, f_{1c}, \ldots$ represent the different conjectures that seller 1 can use.

Starting at the end of time T,

(a) the change in profits $\Delta g_1(T) = g_1(T) - g_1(T - 1)$, and
(b) a set of the prices of different sellers, $p_1(T)$, $p_2(T)$, $p_3(T), \ldots,$

(c) and the change in prices of different sellers, $\Delta p_1(T)$, $\Delta p_2(T)$, $\Delta p_3(T)$, ...

go into the *selector box*, and the selector selects a conjecture function. This is the instant at which the control loop is closed.

The above variables then flow into the selected conjecture box.

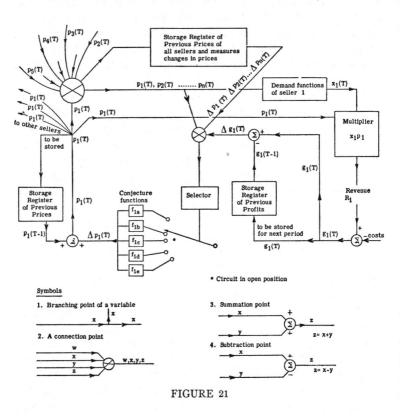

FIGURE 21

The functional relation in the conjecture box works on the variables and produces $\Delta p_1(T + 1)$. With the previous price $p_1(T)$, which was stored in the *storage register of previous prices of seller 1*, the price to be charged by seller 1 at time $T + 1$ is determined and $p_1(T + 1) = p_1(T) + \Delta p_1(T)$. This $p_1(T + 1)$, together with the prices of all the other sellers, $p_2(T + 1)$, $p_3(T + 1)$, ..., determines the sales of seller 1, and these sales multiplied by $p_1(T + 1)$, give his revenue. The costs are regarded as autonomous and Revenue minus Costs gives the profits $g_1(T + 1)$. This value, together with the information on the profits of the previous period given by the *storage register of previous profits*, gives the change in profits $\Delta g_1(T + 1)$. This change in profits, the current prices of all the sellers, and the change in prices of the sellers, all go again into the selector box, which selects another conjecture function. The loop is thus closed once more. The process goes on in cycles as described above for the first cycle.

APPENDIX A

The Motions and Stability of Prices in a Market with Perfect Monopoly

A.1.1. Let us assume that the entrepreneur, in trying to find a price for a product which will enable him to get as much profit as he can, will act as follows:

(1) Any output that he produces, he will produce at the least possible cost.

(2) To this cost, he will add a certain percentage profit markup.

(3) He will change the markup, and the effects on the profits of this change will be the means by which he will decide how to vary his markup. If he increases the markup and finds that his profits are thereby increased, he will go on increasing the price until the profits do not increase any more. Similarly, in decreasing his price, if he finds that the profits are increased, he will continue cutting his price until the profits cease to increase. This kind of approximation will finally lead him to the price where his profits will be maximum.

Mathematically, it means that:

If we let g be the profits and p be the price, g is a function[1] of p, that is, $g = g(p)$, a single-valued function. The entrepreneur is assumed not to know this function: he will merely try to vary his price, and we thus have $p = p(t)$, a continuous monotonic function which in a definite interval passes exactly once through each of the values of p in question. It then follows that $g = g[p(t)] = \psi(t)$.

(A:1) According to condition (3), $\dot{p} = dp/dt \gtrless 0$ according as $dg/dp \gtrless 0$ gives the behavior of our entrepreneur.

Let $\dot{p} = H(g')$, where $g' = dg/dp$ and H is a function. The sufficient condition to satisfy (A:1) is that $H' > 0$ and $H(0) = 0$, where H' means the first derivative $d\dot{p}/dg'$.

A.1.2. The above system, in which time figures only as a differential dt, is said to be autonomous. In such a system, the points where $\dot{p}$ vanishes are called *singular points* and they correspond to states of equilibrium.

In Fig. 23, three states of equilibrium (where $\dot{p} = 0$) of p are possible; these are at points A, B, and C; the state of equilibrium at point A is stable while at B and C it is not. If the price is at position B, the slightest impulse will make it move towards the left or right according to the direction of the

---

[1] The function $g = g(p)$, which represents the structure of our market, is unknown to the entrepreneur.

impulse. At point A, the price will behave quite differently; after the impulse, which displaces p from A, p will move right back to A.

From the above observation, we shall formulate[2] the following definition, in the sense of Liapounoff: "A state of equilibrium is stable whenever, given any region Σ containing it, there is another $\delta(\Sigma)$ in Σ such that any motion starting in the region δ remains in the region Σ."[3] (See Fig. 22.) Whenever these conditions do not hold we have instability. This definition can be stated mathematically as follows:

If $x(t)$ and x_0 represent the value of x after the disturbance and at the state of equilibrium, respectively, we have stability, according to Liapounoff,

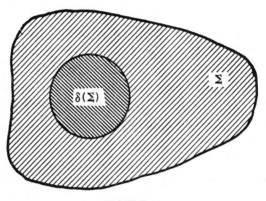

FIGURE 22

whenever for any small positive Σ there exists a positive $\delta(\Sigma)$ such that if at the initial time t_0, $[x(t_0) - x_0] < \delta$, then $[x(t) - x_0] < \Sigma$ for $t \geqq t_0$.

A.1.3. In the system under consideration, we have $\dot{p} = H(g')$, which can also be written

$$\dot{p} = f(p).$$

The point $A(p_0)$ is a singular point[4] where $f(p_0) = 0$. Liapounoff gives a

---

[2] The analysis that follows is based on the following two books: A. A. Andronow and C. E. Chaiken, *Theory of Oscillations* (Princeton: Princeton University Press, 1949); N. Minorsky, *Introduction to Non-linear Mechanics* (Ann Arbor; J. W. Edwards, 1947). This type of technique was introduced to me by Professor Richard M. Goodwin.

[3] Andronow and Chaiken, p. 13.

[4] $A(p_0)$ is a notation meaning a point A, one of whose coordinates is p_0.

definite method for finding out whether our state of equilibrium at $A(p_0)$ is stable or not, when $\dot{p}$ is analytic[5] about p_0.

We are primarily interested in small values of $\xi = p - p_0$. Substituting $p_0 + \xi$ for p in $f(p)$ and expanding it in a Taylor series, we have

$$\dot{\xi} = f(p_0) + \frac{(p - p_0)}{1!} f'(p_0) + \frac{(p - p_0)^2}{2!} f''(p_0) + \cdots$$

$$= f'(p_0)\xi + f''(p_0) \frac{\xi^2}{2!} + \cdots,$$

because $f(p_0) = 0$; we write this

(A:2) $\dot{\xi} = a_1\xi + a_2\xi^2 + \cdots,$

where $a_1 = f'(p_0)$, $a_2 = \frac{1}{2}f''(p_0)$, $\cdots$

Liapounoff's method consists in replacing (A:2) by the linear part[6]

(A:3) $\dot{\xi} = a_1\xi,$

called the equation of the first approximation. The integral of (A:3) is

$$\xi = ce^{\lambda t},$$

where $\lambda = a_1 = f'(p_0)$. Liapounoff states that, if $\lambda < 0$, the equilibrium state is stable; if $\lambda > 0$, the equilibrium is unstable; if $\lambda = 0$, the equation of the first approximation is inadequate for determining stability. Thus Liapounoff affirms that in certain cases the equation obtained by neglecting the nonlinear terms can solve the question of stability of nonlinear equations. Let us now interpret λ in terms of economics:

$$\lambda = a_1 = f'(p_0)$$

$$= \frac{d\xi}{dp_0} = \frac{d\dot{p}}{dp_0} = \frac{d\dot{p}}{dg'} \cdot \frac{dg'}{dp_0}$$

[5] A function $f(x)$ is analytic at the point x_0 whenever it can be expanded in a Taylor series about x_0 (MacLaurin series for $x_0 = 0$), as

$$f(x) = f(x_0) + (x - x_0)f'(x_0) + \frac{(x - x_0)^2}{2!} f''(x_0) + \cdots,$$

where the series is convergent for $(x - x_0)$ sufficiently small. The function $f(x)$ is holomorphic in an interval $b < x < c$, or $-\infty < x < +\infty$, if it is analytic at each point of the interval. Similarly $f(x, y)$ is analytic at the point A (x_0, y_0) if it can be expanded in a Taylor series about A (in powers of $x - x_0$, $y - y_0$) convergent for $(x - x_0)$ and $(y - y_0)$ sufficiently small. It is holomorphic in a region R if it is analytic and single-valued at each point of R. This can be extended to any number of variables.

[6] P. A. Samuelson in his book, *Foundations of Economic Analysis* (Cambridge, Mass.: Harvard University Press, 1947), p. 263, treats the case of competition in a similar way.

because $\dot{p} = H(g')$

$$= H'g_0''$$

Here H' is given as positive and hence the sign of λ depends on g_0''. From the equation $g = g(p)$, when $g_0'' < 0$, profits are maximum and when $g_0'' > 0$, profits are minimum. Hence λ, at the singular point $A(p_0)$, is negative when profits are maximum and positive when profits are minimum.

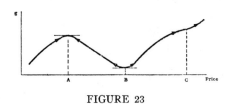

FIGURE 23

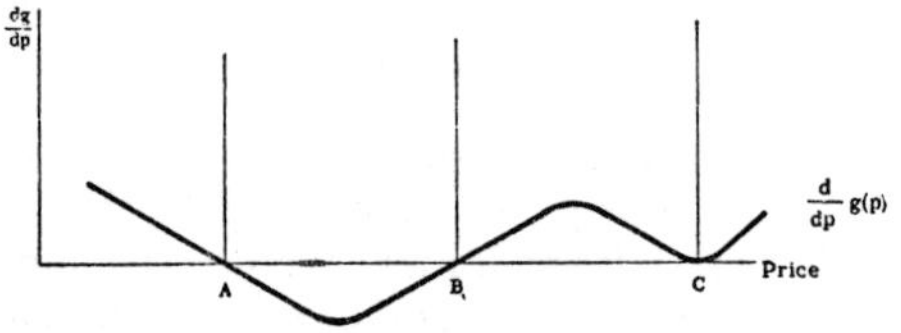

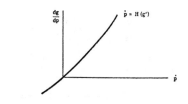

FIGURE 24

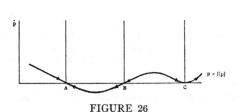

FIGURE 25

FIGURE 26

A.1.4. Graphically, the solution may be derived as shown in Figs. 23, 24, 25 and 26. We may call Fig. 26 (derived from Figs. 23, 24 and 25 as shown in the graphs) a *phase plane*. Figure 26 is obtained by substituting $\dot{p}$ for dg/dp (as given by Fig. 25) in Fig. 24. It is convenient to set $\dot{p}$ equal to $f(p)$, and so the state of the system is determined by the values of the coordinates p and $\dot{p}$, where p is the positional coordinate and $\dot{p}$ the velocity of the system. Thus, for each state of the system there is a corresponding point A with coordinates p and $\dot{p}$; and as time varies, this point A describes a curve called a path, which describes the history of the system. The point $R(p, \dot{p})$ is referred to as the *representative point* of the system. Thus the phase plane represents the totality of all possible states of the given system.

Examining the motion of the representative point along $f(p)$, we find that the movement of the point is always towards the right when $\dot{p} > 0$ and towards the left when $\dot{p} < 0$. This is because $\dot{p}$ is the velocity and a positive velocity corresponds to the increase of the value of p with time, while a negative velocity corresponds to the decrease of p with time.

One may investigate stability directly from the properties of the graph $\dot{p} = f(p)$ near the point (p_0, O). There are three possibilities illustrated by points A, B, and C of Fig. 26. The graph has a negative slope at the point A, $f' < 0$, and we have stability. The second point B corresponds to instability, while at C there is stability on the left and instability on the right. We have here what may be termed *semistable* equilibrium.

APPENDIX B

Maxima and Minima

B.1. *Necessary conditions*

B.1.1. In this appendix, only the necessary conditions for maxima and minima will be given. The proofs for these conditions may be found in any calculus book.

These necessary conditions are satisfied for both a maximum and a minimum of a function. To differentiate between a maximum and a minimum, we need to have sufficient conditions. Because of the dynamic formulation of our approach to the problem, as may be seen in Appendixes A and B, however, we do not need to express the sufficient conditions explicitly to assure us that in the equilibrium state (that is, when the necessary conditions are satisfied) a seller is in a maximum position.

B.1.2. For a function of one variable, $u = f(x)$, a necessary condition for an extreme value (maximum or minimum) of the function at the point X is that $f'(X) = 0$, where $f' = df/dx$.

B.1.3. For a function of n variables, $u = f(x, y, z, \ldots)$, a necessary condition for an extreme value at $X, Y, Z, \ldots$ is that $f_x = f_y = f_z = \cdots = 0$.

B.2. *Maxima and minima with subsidiary conditions*

B.2.1. We will now consider the necessary conditions for the extreme values of functions whose variables are not independent but are connected by one or more relations.

Let us take the problem of maximizing a function

$$(B:1) \qquad u = f(x, y),$$

where x and y are connected by an equation

$$(B:2) \qquad g(x, y) = 0.$$

To solve this problem, if g_y is not zero, we may solve equation (B:2) for y and substitute in equation (B:1), thus obtaining x as the independent variable. A necessary condition for a maximum (or minimum) is that

$$\frac{du}{dx} = f_x - f_y \frac{g_x}{g_y} = 0.$$

The points desired will then be among the simultaneous solutions of the equations

(B:3)   Jacobian $\dfrac{\partial(f, g)}{\partial(x, y)} = 0,$

where $g(x, y) = 0.$

B.2.2. To solve the same problem by the method of Lagrange, let us introduce the Lagrange multiplier λ, forming the function

$$V = f(x, y) + \lambda g(x, y).$$

We now proceed as if x and y were independent variables and set

(B:4) $\dfrac{\partial V}{\partial x} = f_x + \lambda g_x = 0,$

(B:5) $\dfrac{\partial V}{\partial y} = f_y + \lambda g_y = 0.$

Equations (B:2), (B:4), and (B:5) can be solved for the required values of x, y, and λ.

APPENDIX C

The Relationship between the Slopes of the Constant Price Curves and the Partial Derivatives

C.1. From the function $p_1 = F_1(g_1, g_2)$, we find $dp_1 = (\partial F_1/\partial g_1)dg_1 + (\partial F_1/\partial g_2)dg_2$.

For the constant price curve of p_1, p_1 is a parameter; hence $dp_1 = 0$ and the slope of the constant price curve for 1 is

$$(C:1:a) \qquad \left(\frac{dg_2}{dg_1}\right)_{p_1} = -\frac{\partial F_1/\partial g_1}{\partial F_1/\partial g_2}.$$

Similarly from $p_2 = F_2(g_1, g_2)$, the slope of the constant price curve for 2 is

$$(C:1:b) \qquad \left(\frac{dg_2}{dg_1}\right)_{p_2} = -\frac{\partial F_2/\partial g_1}{\partial F_2/\partial g_2}.$$

Now,

$$(C:2:a) \qquad p_1 = F_1(g_1, g_2),$$

$$(C:2:b) \qquad p_2 = F_2(g_1, g_2)$$

are the inverse functions of

$$(C:3:a) \qquad g_1 = g_1(p_1, p_2),$$

$$(C:3:b) \qquad g_2 = g_2(p_1, p_2).$$

In (C:1:a) and (C:1:b), the derivatives dg_2/dg_1 are expressed in terms of the derivatives of the inverse functions; to express them in terms of the original functions, let us now substitute the inverse functions (C:2:a and b) in the given equations (C:3:a and b). We obtain, then, the compound functions

$$(C:4:a) \qquad g_1 = g_1[F_1(g_1, g_2), F_2(g_1, g_2)],$$

$$(C:4:b) \qquad g_2 = g_2[F_1(g_1, g_2), F_2(g_1, g_2)].$$

We now differentiate these equations with respect to g_1 and g_2, regarding p_1 and p_2 as independent variables. If, on the right-hand side, we apply the chain rule for the differentiation of compound functions, we obtain the system of equations

$$1 = \frac{\partial g_1}{\partial p_1} \cdot \frac{\partial F_1}{\partial g_1} + \frac{\partial g_1}{\partial p_2} \cdot \frac{\partial F_2}{\partial g_1}, \qquad 0 = \frac{\partial g_1}{\partial p_1} \cdot \frac{\partial F_1}{\partial g_2} + \frac{\partial g_1}{\partial p_2} \cdot \frac{\partial F_2}{\partial g_2},$$

$$0 = \frac{\partial g_2}{\partial p_1} \cdot \frac{\partial F_1}{\partial g_1} + \frac{\partial g_2}{\partial p_2} \cdot \frac{\partial F_2}{\partial g_1}, \qquad 1 = \frac{\partial g_2}{\partial p_1} \cdot \frac{\partial F_1}{\partial g_2} + \frac{\partial g_2}{\partial p_2} \cdot \frac{\partial F_2}{\partial g_2}.$$

Solving these equations, we obtain

(C:5)

$$\frac{\partial F_1}{\partial g_1} = \frac{\partial g_2 / \partial p_2}{D}, \qquad \frac{\partial F_1}{\partial g_2} = -\frac{\partial g_1 / \partial p_2}{D},$$

$$\frac{\partial F_2}{\partial g_1} = -\frac{\partial g_2 / \partial p_1}{D}, \qquad \frac{\partial F_2}{\partial g_2} = \frac{\partial g_1 / \partial p_1}{D},$$

where

$$D = \begin{vmatrix} \dfrac{\partial g_1}{\partial p_1} & \dfrac{\partial g_1}{\partial p_2} \\[2ex] \dfrac{\partial g_2}{\partial p_1} & \dfrac{\partial g_2}{\partial p_2} \end{vmatrix}$$

This expression D, which we assume is not zero at the point in question, is the *Jacobian* or *functional determinant* of the functions (C:3:a and b) with respect to the variables p_1 and p_2. To denote the Jacobian, let us use the symbol

$$D = \frac{\partial(g_1, g_2)}{\partial(p_1, p_2)}.$$

Substituting the right-hand sides of the equations in (C:5) for the partial derivatives of F with respect to g in (C:1:a and b), we have

(C:6:a)

$$\left(\frac{dg_2}{dg_1} \right)_{p_1} = \frac{\partial g_2 / \partial p_2}{\partial g_1 / \partial p_2},$$

(C:6:b)

$$\left(\frac{dg_2}{dg_1} \right)_{p_2} = \frac{\partial g_2 / \partial p_1}{\partial g_1 / \partial p_1}.$$

We have seen that $\partial g_1 / \partial p_1$, $\partial g_1 / \partial p_2$, $\partial g_2 / \partial p_1$, and $\partial g_2 / \partial p_2$ of Fig. 8 do not change their signs, and this is the sufficient condition that $(dg_2 / dg_1)_{p_1}$ and $(dg_2 / dg_1)_{p_2}$ do not change their signs either.

APPENDIX D

Mathematical Treatment for the Fifth Case in 13.7

D.1. In Fig. 13, the curves are so drawn that the slopes of the constant price curves of p_2 are greater than those of p_1, that is

$$-|(dg_2/dg_1)_{p_2}| > -|(dg_2/dg_1)_{p_1}|$$

or

$$|(dg_2/dg_1)_{p_1}| > |(dg_2/dg_1)_{p_2}|$$

or, from C:6:a and b,

$$\left| \frac{\partial g_2/\partial p_2}{\partial g_1/\partial p_2} \right| > \frac{\partial g_2/\partial p_1}{\partial g_1/\partial p_1}$$

or

(D:1) $$\left| \frac{\partial g_2/\partial p_1}{\partial g_2/\partial p_2} \right| < \frac{\partial g_1/\partial p_1}{\partial g_1/\partial p_2}$$

or $A_2 < A_1$, where A_2 is the left-hand side and A_1 is the right-hand side of (D:1).

Now, the matrix solution for this case is:

$$\begin{bmatrix} dg_1 \\ dg_2 \end{bmatrix} = \begin{bmatrix} -\dfrac{\partial g_1}{\partial p_1} & \dfrac{\partial g_1}{\partial p_2} \\ \dfrac{\partial g_2}{\partial p_1} & -\dfrac{\partial g_2}{\partial p_2} \end{bmatrix} \begin{bmatrix} -dp_1 \\ -dp_2 \end{bmatrix},$$

where dp_1 and dp_2 have negative signs because both the sellers would cut their prices.

For dg_1 to be positive, the following condition must be satisfied:

(D:2) $$\frac{\partial g_1}{\partial p_1} dp_1 > \frac{\partial g_1}{\partial p_2} dp_2$$

or

$$A_1 > \frac{dp_2}{dp_1}.$$

Similarly, for dg_2 to be positive,

(D:3) $$\frac{\partial g_2}{\partial p_1} dp_1 < \frac{\partial g_2}{\partial p_2} dp_2$$

or

$$A_2 < \frac{dp_2}{dp_1}.$$

Condition (D:1) is still valid in the following three equations:

(D:4) $A_2 < A_1 < (dp_2/dp_1),$

(D:5) $A_2 < (dp_2/dp_1) < A_1,$

(D:6) $(dp_2/dp_1) < A_2 < A_1.$

Applying conditions (D:2) and (D:3) in the above equations, we obtain the following results:

in (D:4), $dg_2 > 0,$ $dg_1 < 0;$

in (D:5), $dg_2 > 0,$ $dg_1 > 0;$

in (D:6), $dg_2 < 0,$ $dg_1 > 0.$

In other words, (D:4) means that the sellers will land in region A, (D:5) means that they will land in region B, and (D:6) means that they will land in region C.

As there are no possible combinations other than (D:4), (D:5), and (D:6), we can conclude that they can never reach region D by cutting their prices.

APPENDIX E

Mathematical Treatment for the Sixth Case in 13.8

E.1.1. The graphic solution, showing that, if the two sellers cut their prices, they can land in regions A, C, or D, only, and never in region B, can be proved mathematically as follows:

Because the slopes of the p_1 curves are greater than those of the p_2 curves, (D:1) would now become

$$|(\partial g_2/\partial p_1)/(\partial g_2/\partial p_2)| > |(\partial g_1/\partial p_1)/(\partial g_1/\partial p_2)|$$

or

(E:1)
$$A_2 > A_1.$$

The matrix solution for case 6 would have the same signs as the solution for case 5 if we assume that the sellers cut their prices, and hence (D:2) and (D:3) are valid for case 6.

Condition (E:1) is valid in the following inequalities:

(E:2)
$$A_2 > A_1 > \frac{dp_2}{dp_1},$$

(E:3)
$$A_2 > \frac{dp_2}{dp_1} > A_1,$$

(E:4)
$$\frac{dp_2}{dp_1} > A_2 > A_1.$$

Applying conditions (D:2) and (D:3) in the above inequalities, we derive these results:

in (E:2),	$dg_2 < 0$,	$dg_1 > 0$;
in (E:3),	$dg_2 < 0$,	$dg_1 < 0$;
in (E:4),	$dg_2 > 0$,	$dg_1 < 0$.

In other words, (E:2) means that the sellers will land in region C, (E:3) means that the sellers will land in region D, and (E:4) means that the sellers will land in region A.

If the two sellers cut their prices, all that can result has been described by (E:2), (E:3), and (E:4); hence we know that they can never land in region B.

E.1.2. Let us see what happens to dg_1 and dg_2 if dp_1 and dp_2 are positive, as in the matrix solution in Sec. 13.8.2.

For dg_1 to be positive, we must have

$$\frac{\partial g_1}{\partial p_1} dp_1 < \frac{\partial g_1}{\partial p_2} dp_2$$

or

(E:5) $$A_1 < \frac{dp_2}{dp_1}.$$

Similarly, for dg_2 to be positive, we must have

$$\frac{\partial g_2}{\partial p_1} dp_1 > \frac{\partial g_2}{\partial p_2} dp_2$$

or

(E:6) $$A_2 > \frac{dp_2}{dp_1}.$$

Condition (E:1) is to be satisfied in this case, and for this to be true, we have either (E:2), (E:3), or (E:4).

Applying conditions (E:5) and (E:6) to (E:2), (E:3), and (E:4), we derive the following results:

in (E:2),	$dg_2 > 0,$	$dg_1 < 0;$
in (E:3),	$dg_2 > 0,$	$dg_1 > 0;$
in (E:4),	$dg_2 < 0,$	$dg_1 > 0.$

In other words, (E:2) means that they will land in region A, (E:3) means that they will land in region B, and (E:4) means that they will land in region C.

Thus we see that if both sellers increase their prices they can never land in region D, although they can land in A, B, or C.

APPENDIX F

Constant Profit Curves

Figure 27 represents the constant profit curves for sellers 1 (unbroken lines) and 2 (continuous lines) and also represents the functions of the following form:

$$g_1 = g_1(p_1, p_2),$$

$$g_2 = g_2(p_1, p_2).$$

The curves marked 10.a, 10.b, 10.c, . . . represent the profit curves for seller 1, where 10.a < 10.b < 10.c < $\cdots$; for example, the constant profit curve 10.a shows all the possible combinations of prices p_1 and p_2 that will make the profits of seller 1 constant at 10.a.

The curves marked 20.a, 20.b, 20.c, . . . represent the profit curves for seller 2, where 20.a < 20.b < 20.c < $\cdots$.

In Fig. 27, the curves are drawn so that, in the family of constant profit curves for seller 1, the profit levels of the curves rise as we move upward from the abscissa Op_1, and in the family of constant profit curves for 2, the profit levels of 2 rise as we move to the right from the ordinate Op_2. The minima points (as measured from the abscissa) of the constant profit curves for 1 are connected by the curve VV' and the minima points (as measured from the ordinate) of the constant profit curves for 2 are connected by the curve UU'.

We find that these curves conform to the shapes of the demand and cost curves as generally assumed. Such an example is described in Sec. 13.2.2 and represented in Fig. 5, where it is shown that if we increase the price of seller 1, keeping other sellers' prices constant, the profits of the seller in question increase, reach a maximum, and then decrease. In Fig. 27, keeping 2's price constant and increasing 1's price is equivalent to moving towards the right along a line drawn parallel to the abscissa Op_1. In such a movement we would pass through higher and higher profit curves for seller 1 until we reached VV', after which we would pass through lower and lower profit curves for the same seller.

The curves in Fig. 27 have been drawn on the assumption that the products sold by sellers 1 and 2 are substitutes, that is, that $\partial g_2/\partial p_1 > 0$ and $\partial g_1/\partial p_2 > 0$. Moving to the right along a line drawn parallel to the abscissa (that is, keeping p_2 constant and increasing p_1), we pass through higher and higher profit curves for 2. This means that $\partial g_2/\partial p_1 > 0$. Similarly, moving along a line drawn parallel to the ordinate Op_2, we can see that $\partial g_1/\partial p_2 > 0$.

On the right-hand side of $V'WU$, which lies in the northeast corner of Fig. 27, we find that there are points where the constant profit curves of 1

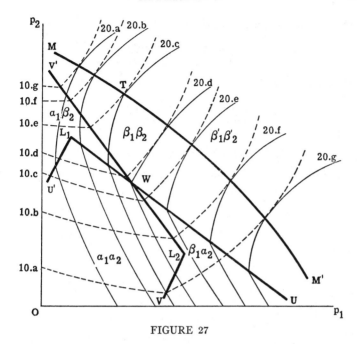

FIGURE 27

and 2 are tangential. Curve MM' is drawn through all such tangential points. The significance of these points can be seen if we move along any constant profit curve; for example, moving along 10.f towards the right we find that we pass through higher and higher constant profit curves for 2 until we reach the tangential point T. After T we pass through lower and lower curves for 2. This means that the joint profits of 1 and 2 first increase and reach a maximum at T, after which the joint profits decrease.

The VV', UU', and MM' curves of Fig. 27 have, respectively, the same properties as vv', uu', and uv' of Fig. 15.

Figure 27 is divided (by heavy lines) into five regions as follows:

$U'WV'$ belongs to region $\alpha_1\beta_2$,

VWU belongs to region $\beta_1\alpha_2$,

$U'WV$ belongs to region $\alpha_1\alpha_2$,

$V'WU$ belongs to region $\beta_1\beta_2$, and the right-hand side of MM' belongs to region $\beta_1'\beta_2'$.

Along the line MM', the slopes of the constant profit curves for both 1 and 2 are equal.

The slope of the constant profit curves of 1 is

$$\left(\frac{dp_2}{dp_1}\right)_{\sigma_1} = -\left(\frac{\partial g_1/\partial p_1}{\partial g_1/\partial p_2}\right).$$

The slope of the constant profit curve of 2 is

$$\left(\frac{dp_2}{dp_1}\right)_{\sigma_2} = -\left(\frac{\partial g_2/\partial p_1}{\partial g_2/\partial p_2}\right).$$

Along the line MM',

$$\left(\frac{\partial g_1/\partial p_1}{\partial g_1/\partial p_2}\right) = \left(\frac{\partial g_2/\partial p_1}{\partial g_2/\partial p_2}\right),$$

that is,

$$(\partial g_1/\partial p_1)(\partial g_2/\partial p_2) - (\partial g_2/\partial p_1)(\partial g_1/\partial p_2) = 0.$$

The left-hand side is the same as the Jacobian D of Appendix C.

A SELECTED BIBLIOGRAPHY

The following bibliography includes only those books and articles that are directly related to the subject matter of this book. Readers seeking an exhaustive bibliography on the Theory of Markets are referred to the lists at the end of Professor Chamberlin's book.

Allen, R. G. D. *Mathematical Economics*. London: Macmillan, 1956. pp. 493–530.

Andronow, A. A., and C. E. Chaiken. *Theory of Oscillations*. Princeton: Princeton University Press, 1949.

Bain, Joe S. "Market Classifications in Modern Price Theory," *Quarterly Journal of Economics*, LVI (1942), pp. 560–574.

Boulding, Kenneth E. *Economic Analysis*. Revised Edition. New York: Harper, 1948.

Bowley, A. L. *The Mathematical Groundwork of Economics*. London: Oxford University Press, 1924.

Brown, Gordon S., and Donald P. Campbell. *Principles of Servomechanisms*. New York: Wiley, 1950. Chapters 1 and 2.

——— "Control Systems," *Scientific American*, 187 (1952), pp. 56–64.

Chamberlin, Edward H. *The Theory of Monopolistic Competition*. 7th ed., Cambridge, Mass: Harvard University Press, 1956.

——— "On the Origin of 'Oligopoly'," *The Economic Journal*, LXVII (1957), pp. 211–218.

Courant, R. *Differential and Integral Calculus*. New York: Nordemann, 1938. Vols. 1 and 2.

Cournot, A. A. *Researches into the Mathematical Principles of the Theory of Wealth*. 1838. Translated by N. T. Bacon and Irving Fisher. New York: Macmillan, 1927.

Dean, Joel. *Managerial Economics*. New York: Prentice-Hall, 1951.

Dorfman, Robert, Paul A. Samuelson and Robert M. Solow. *Linear Programming and Economic Analysis*. New York: McGraw-Hill, 1958. pp. 417–446.

Ellsberg, D. "Theory of the Reluctant Duelist," *American Economic Review*, XLVI (1956), pp. 909–923.

Fellner, William. *Competition Among the Few*. New York: Knopf, 1949.

Hicks, J. R. "Annual Survey of Economic Theory: The Theory of Monopoly," *Econometrica*, III (1935), pp. 1–20.

Hurwicz, Leonid. "The Theory of Economic Behavior," *American Economic Review*, XXXV (1945), pp. 909–925.

Kaysen, Carl. "Dynamic Aspects of Oligopoly Price Theory," *American Economic Review*, XLII (1952), pp. 198–213.

Kaldor, N. "The Equilibrium of the Firm," *Economic Journal*, XLIV (1934), pp. 60–76.

—— "Mrs. Robinson's 'Economics of Imperfect Competition'," *Economica*, I (new series: 1934), pp. 335–341.

Machlup, Fritz. *The Economics of Sellers' Competition:* Model Analysis of Seller's Conduct. Baltimore: Johns Hopkins Press, 1952.

Minorsky, N. *Introduction to Non-linear Mechanics.* Ann Arbor: J. W. Edwards, 1947.

Nichol, A. J. "The Influence of Marginal Buyers on Monopolistic Competition," *The Quarterly Journal of Economics*, XLIX (1935), pp. 121–137.

Oldenbourg, R. C. "Deviation Dependent Step-by-Step Control as Means to Achieve Optimum Control for Plants with Large Distance-velocity Lag," *Conference on Automatic Control*, Cranfield, England, 1951. London: Butterworth's Scientific Publications, 1952. pp. 435–447.

Robinson, Joan. *The Economics of Imperfect Competition.* London: Macmillan, 1933.

—— "Imperfect Competition Revisited," *Economic Journal*, LXIII (1953), pp. 579–593.

Samuelson, Paul A. *Foundations of Economic Analysis.* Cambridge: Harvard University Press, 1950.

Sartorius, Hans. "Deviation Dependent Step-by-Step Control Systems and Their Stability," *Conference on Automatic Control*, Cranfield, England, 1951. London: Butterworth's Scientific Publications, 1952. pp. 421–434.

Schelling, T. C. "An Essay on Bargaining," *American Economic Review.* XLVI (1956), pp. 281–306.

Smithies, A. "Equilibrium in Monopolistic Competition," *Quarterly Journal of Economics*, LV (1940), pp. 95–115.

—— "The Stability of Competitive Equilibrium," *Econometrica*, X (1942), pp. 258–274.

Triffin, Robert. *Monopolistic Competition and General Equilibrium Theory.* Cambridge: Harvard University Press, 1940.

Tustin, A. "Feedback," *Scientific American*, 187 (1952), pp. 48–55.

von Neumann, J., and O. Morgenstern. *Theory of Games and Economic Behavior.* Princeton: Princeton University Press, 1947.

von Stackelberg, H. *Marktform und Gleichgewicht*, Vienna and Berlin, 1934.

Wagner, H. M. "Advances in Game Theory," *American Economic Review*, XLVIII (1958), pp. 368–397.

INDEX